GOD'S
PROMISES
of Abundance for
HEALING

SALLIE DAWKINS

I

God's Promises of Abundance for Healing

LCCN 2022904865

eBook ISBN: 978-1-955861-33-5; Print Paperback ISBN 978-1-955861-34-2

Published by
Firebrand United, LLC
P.O. Box 2506
Danville, Kentucky
40423-2506 USA
www.FirebrandUnited.com

God's Promises of Abundance for Healing

How to Use This Resource   1

Old Testament Scriptures   5

New Testament Scriptures   89

General Index   173

Can You Help?   201

Also by This Author   203

How to Use This Resource

A prayer partner's comment led me to create this book of healing scriptures. The prayer request was for an eye issue. My friend commented that perhaps the real problem was not seeing clearly. He suggested it was a matter of not seeing as God sees. Indeed, in 1 Samuel 16:7, God speaks to Samuel, saying, "I don't see as man sees. For man looks at the outward appearance, but Yahweh looks at the heart." I hadn't been asking God to reveal roots of issues, but isn't it better to deal with the source than with symptoms?

God calls himself "Jehovah Rapha." He is the Lord who heals (Exodus 15:26). Healing is one of the benefits of being a Christian (Psalm 103:2-5). This resource reveals God's will for healing. We fasten our faith to the Word of God. Scripture is our plumb line for aligning our words, our will, and our ways.

Though not a complete list of healing scriptures, it's enough to get you started on your journey of discovery. We chose World English Bible (WEB) translation for this project because it's an easy to understand Public Domain resource available to everyone. I encourage you to look up the healing scriptures in your favorite Bible translations. The slight difference in wording between translations is often very eye-opening.

God's word is eternal, and his instructions and promises for healing have not expired. I would recommend reading each scripture for yourself. Consider highlighting the verses in your Bible for future reference, and remember to read the context of the text from the surrounding scriptures for fuller meaning.

God's word is life and health (Proverbs 4:20-22). Ponder or meditate on how these scriptures might apply to your life. Insert your name into the scripture as if God is speaking directly to you-because He is!

You might re-write the verses, create declarations, or craft personalized prayers to meet your needs. Aligning our words with God's word brings forth healing (Isaiah 55:11, Matthew 8:8).

Allow these scriptures to abide in you (John 15:7) and receive God's supernatural healing for your own life. With Jesus Christ as our Savior and

LORD, sickness and disease have no power over us. We are dead to sin (Romans 6:17) and living a new life in Christ (2 Corinthians 5:17). Our bodies are temples of the Living God (Romans 12:1, 1 Corinthians 3:16). His life permeates every area of our life and restores us to good health (John 6:63). Just as God forgave our sins and trespasses, He commands us to forgive others (Colossians 3:12-13). We overcome the works of the devil by the blood of the Lamb and the words of our testimony (Revelation 12:11).

Praying for your healing, health, and wholeness in every aspect of life,

Sallie Dawkins

Old Testament Scriptures

Genesis 1:27 God created man in his own image. In God's image he created him; male and female he created them.

Genesis 2:24-25 Therefore a man will leave his father and his mother, and will join with his wife, and they will be one flesh. The man and his wife were both naked, and they were not ashamed.

Genesis 4:7 "If you do well, won't it be lifted up? If you don't do well, sin crouches at the door. Its desire is for you, but you are to rule over it."

Genesis 6:3 Yahweh said, "My Spirit will not strive with man forever, because he also is flesh; so his days will be one hundred twenty years."

Genesis 15:1   After these things Yahweh's word came to Abram in a vision, saying, "Don't be afraid, Abram. I am your shield, your exceedingly great reward."

Genesis 15:15   ...but you will go to your fathers in peace. You will be buried at a good old age.

Genesis 18:14   "Is anything too hard for Yahweh? At the set time I will return to you, when the season comes around, and Sarah will have a son."

Genesis 20:17   Abraham prayed to God. So God healed Abimelech, his wife, and his female servants, and they bore children.

Genesis 25:21   Isaac entreated Yahweh for his wife, because she was barren. Yahweh was entreated by him, and Rebekah his wife conceived.

Genesis 32:25   When he saw that he didn't prevail against him, the man touched the hollow of his thigh, and the hollow of Jacob's thigh was strained as he wrestled.

Exodus 4:11-12 Yahweh said to him, "Who made man's mouth? Or who makes one mute, or deaf, or seeing, or blind? Isn't it I, Yahweh? Now therefore go, and I will be with your mouth, and teach you what you shall speak."

Exodus 4:31 The people believed, and when they heard that Yahweh had visited the children of Israel, and that he had seen their affliction, then they bowed their heads and worshiped.

Exodus 12:13 The blood shall be to you for a token on the houses where you are. When I see the blood, I will pass over you, and no plague will be on you to destroy you when I strike the land of Egypt.

Exodus 14:13-14 Moses said to the people, "Don't be afraid. Stand still, and see the salvation of Yahweh, which he will work for you today; for you will never again see the Egyptians whom you have seen today. Yahweh will fight for you, and you shall be still."

Exodus 15:2 Yah is my strength and song. He has become my salvation. This is my God, and I will praise him; my father's God, and I will exalt him.

Exodus 15:26 He said, "If you will diligently listen to Yahweh your God's voice, and will do that which is right in his eyes, and will pay attention to his commandments, and keep all his statutes, I will put none of the diseases on you which I have put on the Egyptians; for I am Yahweh who heals you."

Exodus 23:25 You shall serve Yahweh your God, and he will bless your bread and your water, and I will take sickness away from among you.

Exodus 23:26 No one will miscarry or be barren in your land. I will fulfill the number of your days.

Leviticus 10:9 "You and your sons are not to drink wine or strong drink whenever you go into the Tent of Meeting, or you will die. This shall be a statute forever throughout your generations."

Leviticus 14:53-55 "...So shall he make atonement for the house; and it shall be clean." This is the law for any plague of leprosy, and for an itch, and for the destructive mildew of a garment, and for a house,"

Leviticus 19:17 "You shall not hate your brother in your heart. You shall surely rebuke your neighbor, and not bear sin because of him."

Leviticus 19:28-29 "You shall not make any cuttings in your flesh for the dead, nor tattoo any marks on you. I am Yahweh. Don't profane your daughter, to make her a prostitute; lest the land fall to prostitution, and the land become full of wickedness."

Leviticus 19:30-31 "You shall keep my Sabbaths, and reverence my sanctuary; I am Yahweh. Don't turn to those who are mediums, nor to the wizards. Don't seek them out, to be defiled by them. I am Yahweh your God."

Leviticus 25:10 "You shall make the fiftieth year holy, and proclaim liberty throughout the land to all its inhabitants. It shall be a jubilee to you; and each of you shall return to his own property, and each of you shall return to his family."

Leviticus 25:17 "You shall not wrong one another, but you shall fear your God; for I am Yahweh your God."

Numbers 5:20-22 "But if you have gone astray, being under your husband's authority, and if you are defiled, and some man has lain with you besides your husband—" then the priest shall cause the woman to swear with the oath of cursing, and the priest shall tell the woman, "May Yahweh make you a curse and an oath among your people, when Yahweh allows your thigh to fall away, and your body to swell; and this water that brings a curse will go into your bowels, and make your body swell, and your thigh fall away." The woman shall say, "Amen, Amen."

Numbers 6:26 "Yahweh lift up his face toward you, and give you peace."

Numbers 17:10 Yahweh said to Moses, "Put back the rod of Aaron before the covenant, to be kept for a token against the children of rebellion;

that you may make an end of their complaining against me, that they not die."

Numbers 23:19 God is not a man, that he should lie, nor a son of man, that he should repent. Has he said, and he won't do it? Or has he spoken, and he won't make it good?

Deuteronomy 3:22 "You shall not fear them; for Yahweh your God himself fights for you."

Deuteronomy 5:16 "Honor your father and your mother, as Yahweh your God commanded you; that your days may be long, and that it may go well with you in the land which Yahweh your God gives you."

Deuteronomy 6:4 Hear, Israel: Yahweh is our God. Yahweh is one.

Deuteronomy 7:15 Yahweh will take away from you all sickness; and he will put none of the evil diseases of Egypt, which you know, on you, but will lay them on all those who hate you.

Deuteronomy 11:9 ...and that you may prolong your days in the land which Yahweh swore to your fathers to give to them and to their offspring, a land flowing with milk and honey.

Deuteronomy 21:5 The priests the sons of Levi shall come near, for them Yahweh your God has chosen to minister to him, and to bless in Yahweh's name; and according to their word shall every controversy and every assault be decided.

Deuteronomy 23:5 Nevertheless Yahweh your God wouldn't listen to Balaam, but Yahweh your God turned the curse into a blessing to you, because Yahweh your God loved you.

Deuteronomy 28:1 It shall happen, if you shall listen diligently to Yahweh your God's voice, to observe to do all his commandments which I command you today, that Yahweh your God will set you high above all the nations of the earth.

Deuteronomy 28:15 But it shall come to pass, if you will not listen to Yahweh your God's voice, to observe to do all his commandments and his statutes which I command you today, that all these curses will come on you and overtake you.

Deuteronomy 28:20 Yahweh will send on you cursing, confusion, and rebuke in all that you put your hand to do, until you are destroyed and until you perish quickly, because of the evil of your doings, by which you have forsaken me.

Deuteronomy 28:22 Yahweh will strike you with consumption, with fever, with inflammation, with fiery heat, with the sword, with blight, and with mildew. They will pursue you until you perish.

Deuteronomy 28:28-29 Yahweh will strike you with madness, with blindness, and with astonishment of heart. You will grope at noonday, as the blind gropes in darkness, and you shall not prosper in your ways. You will only be oppressed and robbed always, and there will be no one to save you.

Deuteronomy 28:35 Yahweh will strike you in the knees and in the legs with a sore boil, of which you cannot be healed, from the sole of your foot to the crown of your head.

Deuteronomy 28:47-48 Because you didn't serve Yahweh your God with joyfulness and with gladness of heart, by reason of the abundance of all things; therefore you will serve your enemies whom Yahweh sends against you, in hunger, in thirst, in nakedness, and in lack of all things. He will put an iron yoke on your neck until he has destroyed you.

Deuteronomy 28:58-60 If you will not observe to do all the words of this law that are written in this book, that you may fear this glorious and fearful name, YAHWEH your God, then Yahweh will make your plagues and the plagues of your offspring fearful, even great plagues, and of long duration, and severe sicknesses, and of long duration. He will bring on you again all the diseases of Egypt, which you were afraid of; and they will cling to you.

Deuteronomy 28:65-66 Among these nations you will find no ease, and there will be no rest for the sole of your foot; but Yahweh will give you there a trembling heart, failing of eyes, and pining of soul. Your life will hang in doubt before you. You will be afraid night and day, and will have no assurance of your life.

Deuteronomy 30:19-20 I call heaven and earth to witness against you today that I have set before you life and death, the blessing and the curse. Therefore choose life, that you may live, you and your descendants, to love Yahweh your God, to obey his voice, and to cling to him; for he is your life, and the length of your days, that you may dwell in the land which Yahweh swore to your fathers, to Abraham, to Isaac, and to Jacob, to give them.

Deuteronomy 31:6 "Be strong and courageous. Don't be afraid or scared of them; for Yahweh your God himself is who goes with you. He will not fail you nor forsake you."

Deuteronomy 32:39 "See now that I myself am he. There is no god with me. I kill and I make alive. I wound and I heal. There is no one who can deliver out of my hand."

Deuteronomy 33:12 About Benjamin he said, "The beloved of Yahweh will dwell in safety by him. He covers him all day long. He dwells between his shoulders."

Deuteronomy 33:25 Your bars will be iron and bronze. As your days, so your strength will be.

Deuteronomy 34:7 Moses was one hundred twenty years old when he died. His eye was not dim, nor his strength gone.

Joshua 1:9 "Haven't I commanded you? Be strong and courageous. Don't be afraid. Don't be dismayed, for Yahweh your God is with you wherever you go."

Joshua 21:45 Nothing failed of any good thing which Yahweh had spoken to the house of Israel. All came to pass.

1 Samuel 1:4-5 When the day came that Elkanah sacrificed, he gave portions to Peninnah his wife and to all her sons and her daughters; but he gave a double portion to Hannah, for he loved Hannah, but Yahweh had shut up her womb.

1 Samuel 2:9-10 He will keep the feet of his holy ones, but the wicked will be put to silence in darkness; for no man will prevail by strength. Those who strive with Yahweh shall be broken to pieces. He will thunder against them in the sky. "Yahweh will judge the ends of the earth. He will give strength to his king, and exalt the horn of his anointed."

1 Samuel 6:3 They said, "If you send away the ark of the God of Israel, don't send it empty; but by all means return a trespass offering to him. Then you will be healed, and it will be known to you why his hand is not removed from you."

1 Samuel 15:23 "For rebellion is as the sin of witchcraft, and stubbornness is as idolatry and teraphim. Because you have rejected Yahweh's word, he has also rejected you from being king."

1 Samuel 16:7 But Yahweh said to Samuel, "Don't look on his face, or on the height of his stature, because I have rejected him; for I don't see as man sees. For man looks at the outward appearance, but Yahweh looks at the heart."

1 Samuel 23:16 Jonathan, Saul's son, arose, and went to David into the woods, and strengthened his hand in God.

2 Samuel 22:37 You have enlarged my steps under me. My feet have not slipped.

2 Samuel 22:49 ...who brings me away from my enemies. Yes, you lift me up above those who rise up against me. You deliver me from the violent man.

1 Kings 8:37-39 "If there is famine in the land, if there is pestilence, if there is blight, mildew, locust or caterpillar; if their enemy besieges them in the land of their cities; whatever plague, whatever sickness there is; whatever prayer and supplication is made by any man, or by all your people Israel, who shall each know the plague of his own heart, and spread out his hands toward this house, then hear in heaven, your dwelling place, and forgive, and act, and give to every man according to all his ways, whose heart you know (for you, even you only, know the hearts of all the children of men);"

1 Kings 8:56 "Blessed be Yahweh, who has given rest to his people Israel, according to all that he promised. There has not failed one word of all his good promise, which he promised by Moses his servant."

2 Kings 2:21-22 He went out to the spring of the waters, and threw salt into it, and said, "Yahweh says, 'I have healed these waters. There shall not be from there any more death or barren wasteland.'" So the waters were healed to this day, according to Elisha's word which he spoke.

2 Kings 4:19, 32, 33 He said to his father, "My head! My head!" He said to his servant, "Carry him to his mother." When Elisha had come into the house, behold, the child was dead, and lying on his bed. He went in therefore, and shut the door on them both, and prayed to Yahweh.

2 Kings 4:35 Then he returned, and walked in the house once back and forth; and went up, and stretched himself out on him. Then the child sneezed seven times, and the child opened his eyes.

2 Kings 6:17 Elisha prayed, and said, "Yahweh, please open his eyes, that he may see." Yahweh opened the young man's eyes; and he saw: and behold, the mountain was full of horses and chariots of fire around Elisha.

2 Kings 20:5 "Turn back, and tell Hezekiah the prince of my people, 'Yahweh, the God of David your father, says, "I have heard your prayer. I have seen your tears. Behold, I will heal you. On the third day, you will go up to Yahweh's house.'"

1 Chronicles 4:10 Jabez called on the God of Israel, saying, "Oh that you would bless me indeed, and enlarge my border! May your hand be with me, and may you keep me from evil, that I may not cause pain!" God granted him that which he requested.

1 Chronicles 10:13-14 So Saul died for his trespass which he committed against Yahweh, because of Yahweh's word, which he didn't keep; and also because he asked counsel of one who had a familiar spirit, to inquire, and didn't inquire of Yahweh. Therefore he killed him, and turned the kingdom over to David the son of Jesse.

1 Chronicles 29:11-12   Yours, Yahweh, is the greatness, the power, the glory, the victory, and the majesty! For all that is in the heavens and in the earth is yours. Yours is the kingdom, Yahweh, and you are exalted as head above all. Both riches and honor come from you, and you rule over all! In your hand is power and might! It is in your hand to make great, and to give strength to all!

2 Chronicles 7:14   "...if my people, who are called by my name, will humble themselves, pray, seek my face, and turn from their wicked ways, then I will hear from heaven, will forgive their sin, and will heal their land."

2 Chronicles 16:12   In the thirty-ninth year of his reign, Asa was diseased in his feet. His disease was exceedingly great: yet in his disease he didn't seek Yahweh, but just the physicians.

2 Chronicles 18:26   "...and say, 'The king says, "Put this fellow in the prison, and feed him with bread of affliction and with water of affliction, until I return in peace."'"

2 Chronicles 21:15 "...and you will have great sickness with a disease of your bowels, until your bowels fall out by reason of the sickness, day by day."

2 Chronicles 30:20 Yahweh listened to Hezekiah, and healed the people.

Nehemiah 8:10 Then he said to them, "Go your way. Eat the fat, drink the sweet, and send portions to him for whom nothing is prepared, for today is holy to our Lord. Don't be grieved, for the joy of Yahweh is your strength."

Nehemiah 9:2 The offspring of Israel separated themselves from all foreigners and stood and confessed their sins and the iniquities of their fathers.

Esther 6:1 On that night, the king couldn't sleep. He commanded the book of records of the chronicles to be brought, and they were read to the king.

Job 2:7 So Satan went out from the presence of Yahweh, and struck Job with painful sores from the sole of his foot to his head.

Job 5:17 "Behold, happy is the man whom God corrects. Therefore do not despise the chastening of the Almighty."

Job 5:18 For he wounds and binds up. He injures and his hands make whole.

Job 5:26 You will come to your grave in a full age, like a shock of grain comes in its season.

Job 6:2 "Oh that my anguish were weighed, and all my calamity laid in the balances!"

Job 6:14 "To him who is ready to faint, kindness should be shown from his friend; even to him who forsakes the fear of the Almighty."

Job 10:11-12 You have clothed me with skin and flesh, and knit me together with bones and sinews.

You have granted me life and loving kindness. Your visitation has preserved my spirit.

Job 11:14-16 If iniquity is in your hand, put it far away. Don't let unrighteousness dwell in your tents. Surely then you will lift up your face without spot; Yes, you will be steadfast, and will not fear: for you will forget your misery. You will remember it like waters that have passed away.

Job 17:7 My eye also is dim by reason of sorrow. All my members are as a shadow.

Job 19:20 My bones stick to my skin and to my flesh. I have escaped by the skin of my teeth.

Job 22:28 You will also decree a thing, and it will be established to you. Light will shine on your ways.

Job 27:3-4 ...(for the length of my life is still in me, and the spirit of God is in my nostrils); surely my lips will not speak unrighteousness, neither will my tongue utter deceit.

Job 30:30 My skin grows black and peels from me. My bones are burned with heat.

Job 33:4 The Spirit of God has made me, and the breath of the Almighty gives me life.

Job 33:14-16 For God speaks once, yes twice, though man pays no attention. In a dream, in a vision of the night, when deep sleep falls on men, in slumbering on the bed; Then he opens the ears of men, and seals their instruction,

Job 33:24-25 "...then God is gracious to him, and says, 'Deliver him from going down to the pit, I have found a ransom.' His flesh will be fresher than a child's. He returns to the days of his youth."

Job 34:28 ...so that they caused the cry of the poor to come to him. He heard the cry of the afflicted.

Job 36:8-10 If they are bound in fetters, and are taken in the cords of afflictions, then he shows them their work, and their transgressions, that they have behaved themselves proudly. He also opens their ears to instruction, and commands that they return from iniquity.

Job 38:36 Who has put wisdom in the inward parts? Or who has given understanding to the mind?

Job 41:34 "He sees everything that is high. He is king over all the sons of pride."

Psalm 1:1-2 Blessed is the man who doesn't walk in the counsel of the wicked, nor stand on the path of sinners, nor sit in the seat of scoffers; but his delight is in Yahweh's law. On his law he meditates day and night.

Psalm 4:4 Stand in awe, and don't sin. Search your own heart on your bed, and be still. Selah.

Psalm 4:8 In peace I will both lay myself down and sleep, for you, Yahweh alone, make me live in safety.

Psalm 5:9 For there is no faithfulness in their mouth. Their heart is destruction. Their throat is an open tomb. They flatter with their tongue.

Psalm 5:11 But let all those who take refuge in you rejoice. Let them always shout for joy, because you defend them. Let them also who love your name be joyful in you.

Psalm 6:2 Have mercy on me, Yahweh, for I am faint. Yahweh, heal me, for my bones are troubled.

Psalm 7:14-16 Behold, he travails with iniquity. Yes, he has conceived mischief, and brought out falsehood. He has dug a hole, and has fallen into the pit which he made. The trouble he causes shall return to his own head. His violence shall come down on the crown of his own head.

Psalm 11:4 Yahweh is in his holy temple. Yahweh is on his throne in heaven. His eyes observe. His eyes examine the children of men.

Psalm 12:2-4 Everyone lies to his neighbor. They speak with flattering lips, and with a double heart.

May Yahweh cut off all flattering lips, and the tongue that boasts, who have said, "With our tongue we will prevail. Our lips are our own. Who is lord over us?"

Psalm 12:5 "Because of the oppression of the weak and because of the groaning of the needy, I will now arise," says Yahweh; "I will set him in safety from those who malign him."

Psalm 16:9 Therefore my heart is glad, and my tongue rejoices. My body shall also dwell in safety.

Psalm 16:11 You will show me the path of life. In your presence is fullness of joy. In your right hand there are pleasures forever more.

Psalm 17:5 My steps have held fast to your paths. My feet have not slipped.

Psalm 17:9-10 ...from the wicked who oppress me, my deadly enemies, who surround me. They close up their callous hearts. With their mouth they speak proudly.

Psalm 17:15 As for me, I shall see your face in righteousness. I shall be satisfied, when I awake, with seeing your form.

Psalm 18:1-3 I love you, Yahweh, my strength. Yahweh is my rock, my fortress, and my deliverer; my God, my rock, in whom I take refuge; my shield, and the horn of my salvation, my high tower. I call on Yahweh, who is worthy to be praised; and I am saved from my enemies.

Psalm 18:28-30 For you will light my lamp, Yahweh. My God will light up my darkness. For by you, I advance through a troop. By my God, I leap over a wall. As for God, his way is perfect. Yahweh's word is tried. He is a shield to all those who take refuge in him.

Psalm 18:32-34 ...the God who arms me with strength, and makes my way perfect? He makes my feet like deer's feet, and sets me on my high places. He teaches my hands to war, so that my arms bend a bow of bronze.

Psalm 18:48 He rescues me from my enemies. Yes, you lift me up above those who rise up against me. You deliver me from the violent man.

Psalm 19:12 Who can discern his errors? Forgive me from hidden errors.

Psalm 19:14 Let the words of my mouth and the meditation of my heart be acceptable in your sight, Yahweh, my rock, and my redeemer.

Psalm 22:14 I am poured out like water. All my bones are out of joint. My heart is like wax. It is melted within me.

Psalm 23:2-3 He makes me lie down in green pastures. He leads me beside still waters. He restores my soul. He guides me in the paths of righteousness for his name's sake.

Psalm 23:4 Even though I walk through the valley of the shadow of death, I will fear no evil, for you are with me. Your rod and your staff, they comfort me.

Psalm 23:5 You prepare a table before me in the presence of my enemies. You anoint my head with oil. My cup runs over.

Psalm 23:6 Surely goodness and loving kindness shall follow me all the days of my life, and I will dwell in Yahweh's house forever.

Psalm 24:6 This is the generation of those who seek Him, who seek your face—even Jacob. Selah.

Psalm 25:2 My God, I have trusted in you. Don't let me be shamed. Don't let my enemies triumph over me.

Psalm 25:7 Don't remember the sins of my youth, nor my transgressions. Remember me according to your loving kindness, for your goodness' sake, Yahweh.

Psalm 25:15 My eyes are ever on Yahweh, for he will pluck my feet out of the net.

Psalm 25:18 Consider my affliction and my travail. Forgive all my sins.

Psalm 25:20-22 Oh keep my soul, and deliver me. Let me not be disappointed, for I take refuge in you. Let integrity and uprightness preserve me, for I wait for you. God, redeem Israel out of all his troubles.

Psalm 26:6-7 I will wash my hands in innocence, so I will go about your altar, Yahweh, that I may make the voice of thanksgiving to be heard and tell of all your wondrous deeds.

Psalm 27:1-2 Yahweh is my light and my salvation. Whom shall I fear? Yahweh is the strength of my life. Of whom shall I be afraid? When evildoers came at me to eat up my flesh, even my adversaries and my foes, they stumbled and fell.

Psalm 27:3 Though an army should encamp against me, my heart shall not fear. Though war should rise against me, even then I will be confident.

Psalm 29:11 Yahweh will give strength to his people. Yahweh will bless his people with peace.

Psalm 30:1-2 I will extol you, Yahweh, for you have raised me up, and have not made my foes to rejoice over me. Yahweh my God, I cried to you, and you have healed me.

Psalm 30:11 You have turned my mourning into dancing for me. You have removed my sackcloth, and clothed me with gladness,

Psalm 31:10 For my life is spent with sorrow, my years with sighing. My strength fails because of my iniquity. My bones are wasted away.

Psalm 31:23-24 Oh love Yahweh, all you his saints! Yahweh preserves the faithful, and fully recompenses him who behaves arrogantly. Be strong, and let your heart take courage, all you who hope in Yahweh.

Psalm 32:1-2 Blessed is he whose disobedience is forgiven, whose sin is covered. Blessed is the man to whom Yahweh doesn't impute iniquity, in whose spirit there is no deceit.

Psalm 32:3-5 When I kept silence, my bones wasted away through my groaning all day long. For day and night your hand was heavy on me. My strength was sapped in the heat of summer. Selah. I acknowledged my sin to you. I didn't hide my iniquity. I said, I will confess my transgressions to Yahweh, and you forgave the iniquity of my sin. Selah.

Psalm 32:10-11 Many sorrows come to the wicked, but loving kindness shall surround him who trusts in Yahweh. Be glad in Yahweh, and rejoice, you righteous! Shout for joy, all you who are upright in heart!

Psalm 33:18-19 Behold, Yahweh's eye is on those who fear him, on those who hope in his loving kindness, to deliver their soul from death, to keep them alive in famine.

Psalm 34:4 I sought Yahweh, and he answered me, and delivered me from all my fears.

Psalm 34:7 Yahweh's angel encamps around those who fear him, and delivers them.

Psalm 34:15-16 Yahweh's eyes are toward the righteous. His ears listen to their cry. Yahweh's face is against those who do evil, to cut off their memory from the earth.

Psalm 34:18 Yahweh is near to those who have a broken heart, and saves those who have a crushed spirit.

Psalm 34:19 Many are the afflictions of the righteous, but Yahweh delivers him out of them all.

Psalm 34:20 He protects all of his bones. Not one of them is broken.

Psalm 35:9-10 My soul shall be joyful in Yahweh. It shall rejoice in his salvation. All my bones shall say, "Yahweh, who is like you, who delivers the poor from him who is too strong for him; yes, the poor and the needy from him who robs him?"[]

Psalm 37:7-9 Rest in Yahweh, and wait patiently for him. Don't fret because of him who prospers in his way, because of the man who makes wicked plots happen. Cease from anger, and forsake wrath. Don't fret; it leads only to evildoing. For evildoers shall be cut off, but those who wait for Yahweh shall inherit the land.

Psalm 37:24 Though he stumble, he shall not fall, for Yahweh holds him up with his hand.

Psalm 38:3 There is no soundness in my flesh because of your indignation, neither is there any health in my bones because of my sin.

Psalm 38:4-5 For my iniquities have gone over my head. As a heavy burden, they are too heavy for me. My wounds are loathsome and corrupt because of my foolishness.

Psalm 38:7 For my waist is filled with burning. There is no soundness in my flesh.

Psalm 38:17-18 For I am ready to fall. My pain is continually before me. For I will declare my iniquity. I will be sorry for my sin.

Psalm 39:2-3 I was mute with silence. I held my peace, even from good. My sorrow was stirred. My heart was hot within me. While I meditated, the fire burned. I spoke with my tongue:

Psalm 39:4-5 "Yahweh, show me my end, what is the measure of my days. Let me know how frail I am. Behold, you have made my days hand widths. My lifetime is as nothing before you. Surely every man stands as a breath." Selah.

Psalm 39:10-11 "Remove your scourge away from me. I am overcome by the blow of your hand. When you rebuke and correct man for iniquity, you consume his wealth like a moth. Surely every man is but a breath." Selah.

Psalm 40:2-3 He brought me up also out of a horrible pit, out of the miry clay. He set my feet on a rock, and gave me a firm place to stand. He has put a new song in my mouth, even praise to our God. Many shall see it, and fear, and shall trust in Yahweh.

Psalm 41:2 Yahweh will preserve him, and keep him alive. He shall be blessed on the earth, and he will not surrender him to the will of his enemies.

Psalm 41:3-4 Yahweh will sustain him on his sickbed, and restore him from his bed of illness. I said, "Yahweh, have mercy on me! Heal me, for I have sinned against you."

Psalm 43:5 Why are you in despair, my soul? Why are you disturbed within me? Hope in God! For I shall still praise him: my Savior, my helper, and my God.

Psalm 45:7 You have loved righteousness, and hated wickedness. Therefore God, your God, has anointed you with the oil of gladness above your fellows.

Psalm 51:5-6 Behold, I was born in iniquity. My mother conceived me in sin. Behold, you desire truth in the inward parts. You teach me wisdom in the inmost place.

Psalm 51:8 Let me hear joy and gladness, that the bones which you have broken may rejoice.

Psalm 51:10 Create in me a clean heart, O God. Renew a right spirit within me.

Psalm 55:4-5 My heart is severely pained within me. The terrors of death have fallen on me.- Fearfulness and trembling have come on me. Horror has overwhelmed me.

Psalm 55:22 Cast your burden on Yahweh and he will sustain you. He will never allow the righteous to be moved.

Psalm 56:3 When I am afraid, I will put my trust in you.

Psalm 56:13 For you have delivered my soul from death, and prevented my feet from falling, that I may walk before God in the light of the living.

Psalm 61:2 From the end of the earth, I will call to you when my heart is overwhelmed. Lead me to the rock that is higher than I.

Psalm 63:3-4 Because your loving kindness is better than life, my lips shall praise you. So I will bless you while I live. I will lift up my hands in your name.

Psalm 63:5 My soul shall be satisfied as with the richest food. My mouth shall praise you with joyful lips,

Psalm 66:16-19 Come and hear, all you who fear God. I will declare what he has done for my soul. I cried to him with my mouth. He was extolled with my tongue. If I cherished sin in my heart, the Lord wouldn't have listened. But most certainly, God has listened. He has heard the voice of my prayer.

Psalm 69:20 Reproach has broken my heart, and I am full of heaviness. I looked for some to take pity, but there was none; for comforters, but I found none.

Psalm 69:29 But I am in pain and distress. Let your salvation, God, protect me.

Psalm 71:20-21 You, who have shown us many and bitter troubles, you will let me live. You will bring us up again from the depths of the earth. Increase my honor and comfort me again.

Psalm 72:7 In his days, the righteous shall flourish, and abundance of peace, until the moon is no more.

Psalm 72:14 He will redeem their soul from oppression and violence. Their blood will be precious in his sight.

Psalm 73:2 But as for me, my feet were almost gone. My steps had nearly slipped.

Psalm 73:6 Therefore pride is like a chain around their neck. Violence covers them like a garment.

Psalm 73:21 For my soul was grieved. I was embittered in my heart.

Psalm 73:26 My flesh and my heart fails, but God is the strength of my heart and my portion forever.

Psalm 73:28 But it is good for me to come close to God. I have made the Lord Yahweh my refuge, that I may tell of all your works.

Psalm 77:3 I remember God, and I groan. I complain, and my spirit is overwhelmed. Selah.

Psalm 78:36-42 But they flattered him with their mouth, and lied to him with their tongue. For their heart was not right with him, neither were they faithful in his covenant. But he, being merciful, forgave iniquity, and didn't destroy them. Yes, many times he turned his anger away, and didn't stir up all his wrath. He remembered that they were but flesh, a wind that passes away, and doesn't come again. How often they rebelled against him in the wilderness, and grieved him in the desert! They turned again and tempted God, and provoked the Holy One of Israel. They didn't remember his hand, nor the day when he redeemed them from the adversary;

Psalm 81:11-12 "But my people didn't listen to my voice. Israel desired none of me. So I let them go after the stubbornness of their hearts, that they might walk in their own counsels."

Psalm 89:20-23 " I have found David, my servant. I have anointed him with my holy oil, with whom my hand shall be established. My arm will also strengthen him. No enemy will tax him. No wicked man will oppress him. I will beat down his adversaries before him, and strike those who hate him."

Psalm 89:31-32 "...if they break my statutes, and don't keep my commandments; then I will punish their sin with the rod, and their iniquity with stripes."

Psalm 89:34 "I will not break my covenant, nor alter what my lips have uttered."

Psalm 90:10 The days of our years are seventy, or even by reason of strength eighty years; yet their pride is but labor and sorrow, for it passes quickly, and we fly away.

Psalm 91:5-6 You shall not be afraid of the terror by night, nor of the arrow that flies by day, nor of the pestilence that walks in darkness, nor of the destruction that wastes at noonday.

Psalm 91:10 "...no evil shall happen to you, neither shall any plague come near your dwelling."

Psalm 91:11-12 For he will put his angels in charge of you, to guard you in all your ways. They will bear you up in their hands, so that you won't dash your foot against a stone.

Psalm 91:16 "I will satisfy him with long life, and show him my salvation."

Psalm 92:14 They will still produce fruit in old age. They will be full of sap and green,

Psalm 94:19 In the multitude of my thoughts within me, your comforts delight my soul.

Psalm 95:8-9 Don't harden your heart, as at Meribah, as in the day of Massah in the wilderness, when your fathers tempted me, tested me, and saw my work.

Psalm 101:3 I will set no vile thing before my eyes. I hate the deeds of faithless men. They will not cling to me.

Psalm 102:3-5 For my days consume away like smoke. My bones are burned as a torch. My heart is blighted like grass, and withered, for I forget to eat my bread. By reason of the voice of my groaning, my bones stick to my skin.

Psalm 103:2 Praise Yahweh, my soul, and don't forget all his benefits,

Psalm 103:3 ...who forgives all your sins, who heals all your diseases,

Psalm 103:4-5 ...who redeems your life from destruction, who crowns you with loving kindness and tender mercies, who satisfies your desire with good things, so that your youth is renewed like the eagle's.

Psalm 103:12 As far as the east is from the west, so far has he removed our transgressions from us.

Psalm 103:13-14 Like a father has compassion on his children, so Yahweh has compassion on those who fear him. For he knows how we are made. He remembers that we are dust.

Psalm 103:19 Yahweh has established his throne in the heavens. His kingdom rules over all.

Psalm 103:20-21 Praise Yahweh, you angels of his, who are mighty in strength, who fulfill his word, obeying the voice of his word. Praise Yahweh, all you armies of his, you servants of his, who do his pleasure.

Psalm 104:4 He makes his messengers winds, and his servants flames of fire.

Psalm 104:14-15 He causes the grass to grow for the livestock, and plants for man to cultivate, that he may produce food out of the earth: wine that makes the heart of man glad, oil to make his face to shine, and bread that strengthens man's heart.

Psalm 105:37 He brought them out with silver and gold. There was not one feeble person among his tribes.

Psalm 106:4-5 Remember me, Yahweh, with the favor that you show to your people. Visit me with your salvation, that I may see the prosperity of your chosen, that I may rejoice in the gladness of your nation, that I may glory with your inheritance.

Psalm 106:24-25 Yes, they despised the pleasant land. They didn't believe his word, but murmured in their tents, and didn't listen to Yahweh's voice.

Psalm 107:20 He sends his word, and heals them, and delivers them from their graves.

Psalm 107:27-28 They reel back and forth, and stagger like a drunken man, and are at their wits' end. Then they cry to Yahweh in their trouble, and he brings them out of their distress.

Psalm 109:17-18 Yes, he loved cursing, and it came to him. He didn't delight in blessing, and it was far from him. He clothed himself also with cursing as with his garment. It came into his inward parts like water, like oil into his bones.

Psalm 109:22-24 ...for I am poor and needy. My heart is wounded within me. I fade away like an evening shadow. I am shaken off like a locust. My knees are weak through fasting. My body is thin and lacks fat.

Psalm 112:7-8 He will not be afraid of evil news. His heart is steadfast, trusting in Yahweh. His heart is established. He will not be afraid in the end when he sees his adversaries.

Palm 113:9 He settles the barren woman in her home as a joyful mother of children. Praise Yah!

Psalm 116:3-4 The cords of death surrounded me, the pains of Sheol got a hold of me. I found trouble and sorrow. Then I called on Yahweh's name: "Yahweh, I beg you, deliver my soul."

Psalm 116:8-9 For you have delivered my soul from death, my eyes from tears, and my feet from falling. I will walk before Yahweh in the land of the living.

Psalm 118:6-7 Yahweh is on my side. I will not be afraid. What can man do to me? Yahweh is on my side among those who help me. Therefore I will look in triumph at those who hate me.

Psalm 118:17 I will not die, but live, and declare Yah's works.

Psalm 119:18 Open my eyes, that I may see wondrous things out of your law.

Psalm 119:25 My soul is laid low in the dust. Revive me according to your word!

Psalm 119:28 My soul is weary with sorrow: strengthen me according to your word.

Psalm 119:32 I run in the path of your commandments, for you have set my heart free.

Psalm 119:37 Turn my eyes away from looking at worthless things. Revive me in your ways.

Psalm 119:50 This is my comfort in my affliction, for your word has revived me.

Psalm 119:65-67 You have treated your servant well, according to your word, Yahweh. Teach me good judgment and knowledge, for I believe in your commandments. Before I was afflicted, I went astray; but now I observe your word.

Psalm 119:93 I will never forget your precepts, for with them, you have revived me.

Psalm 119:113 I hate double-minded men, but I love your law.

Psalm 119:153 Consider my affliction, and deliver me, for I don't forget your law.

Psalm 119:170-173 Let my supplication come before you. Deliver me according to your word.- Let my lips utter praise, for you teach me your statutes. Let my tongue sing of your word, for all your commandments are righteousness. Let your hand be ready to help me, for I have chosen your precepts.

Psalm 121:1-2 I will lift up my eyes to the hills. Where does my help come from? My help comes from Yahweh, who made heaven and earth.

Psalm 127:2 It is vain for you to rise up early, to stay up late, eating the bread of toil, for he gives sleep to his loved ones.

Psalm 127:3 Behold, children are a heritage of Yahweh. The fruit of the womb is his reward.

Psalm 139:13 For you formed my inmost being. You knit me together in my mother's womb.

Psalm 139:16 Your eyes saw my body. In your book they were all written, the days that were ordained for me, when as yet there were none of them.

Psalm 139:23-24 Search me, God, and know my heart. Try me, and know my thoughts. See if there is any wicked way in me, and lead me in the everlasting way.

Psalm 140:12 I know that Yahweh will maintain the cause of the afflicted, and justice for the needy.

Psalm 143:3-4 For the enemy pursues my soul. He has struck my life down to the ground. He has made me live in dark places, as those who have been long dead. Therefore my spirit is overwhelmed within me. My heart within me is desolate.

Psalm 143:7-8 Hurry to answer me, Yahweh. My spirit fails. Don't hide your face from me, so that I don't become like those who go down into the pit. Cause me to hear your loving kindness in the morning, for I trust in you. Cause me to know the way in which I should walk, for I lift up my soul to you.

Psalm 145:15-16 The eyes of all wait for you. You give them their food in due season. You open your hand, and satisfy the desire of every living thing.

Psalm 145:21 My mouth will speak the praise of Yahweh. Let all flesh bless his holy name forever and ever.

Psalm 146:7 ...who executes justice for the oppressed; who gives food to the hungry. Yahweh frees the prisoners.

Psalm 146:8 Yahweh opens the eyes of the blind. Yahweh raises up those who are bowed down. Yahweh loves the righteous.

Psalm 147:3 He heals the broken in heart, and binds up their wounds.

Psalm 149:6-9 May the high praises of God be in their mouths, and a two-edged sword in their hand, to execute vengeance on the nations, and punishments on the peoples; to bind their kings with chains, and their nobles with fetters of iron; to execute on them the written judgment. All his saints have this honor. Praise Yah!

Proverbs 3:5-6 Trust in Yahweh with all your heart, and don't lean on your own understanding. In all your ways acknowledge him, and he will make your paths straight.

Proverbs 3:7-8 Don't be wise in your own eyes. Fear Yahweh, and depart from evil. It will be health to your body, and nourishment to your bones.

Proverbs 3:21-23 My son, let them not depart from your eyes. Keep sound wisdom and discretion: so they will be life to your soul, and grace for your neck. Then you shall walk in your way securely. Your foot won't stumble.

Proverbs 3:24 Then you lie down, you will not be afraid. Yes, you will lie down, and your sleep will be sweet.

Proverbs 4:10 Listen, my son, and receive my sayings. The years of your life will be many.

Proverbs 4:20-22 My son, attend to my words. Turn your ear to my sayings. Let them not depart from your eyes. Keep them in the center of your heart. For they are life to those who find them, and health to their whole body.

Proverbs 4:24-25 Put away from yourself a perverse mouth. Put corrupt lips far from you. Let your eyes look straight ahead. Fix your gaze directly before you.

Proverbs 6:20-22 My son, keep your father's commandment, and don't forsake your mother's teaching. Bind them continually on your heart. Tie them around your neck. When you walk, it will lead you. When you sleep, it will watch over you. When you awake, it will talk with you.

Proverbs 6:28-29 Or can one walk on hot coals, and his feet not be scorched? So is he who goes in to his neighbor's wife. Whoever touches her will not be unpunished.

Proverbs 7:23 Until an arrow strikes through his liver, as a bird hurries to the snare, and doesn't know that it will cost his life.

Proverbs 9:6 "Leave your simple ways, and live. Walk in the way of understanding."

Proverbs 10:10 One winking with the eye causes sorrow, but a chattering fool will fall.

Proverbs 10:12 The mouth of the righteous is a spring of life, but violence covers the mouth of the wicked.

Proverbs 10:18-20 He who hides hatred has lying lips. He who utters a slander is a fool. In the multitude of words there is no lack of disobedience, he who restrains his lips does wisely. The tongue of the righteous is like choice silver. The heart of the wicked is of little worth.

Proverbs 12:1 Whoever loves correction loves knowledge, but he who hates reproof is stupid.

Proverbs 12:4 A worthy woman is the crown of her husband, but a disgraceful wife is as rottenness in his bones.

Proverbs 12:8 A man shall be commended according to his wisdom, but he who has a warped mind shall be despised.

Proverbs 12:13-14 An evil man is trapped by sinfulness of lips, but the righteous shall come out of trouble. A man shall be satisfied with good by the fruit of his mouth. The work of a man's hands shall be rewarded to him.

Proverbs 12:15-16 The way of a fool is right in his own eyes, but he who is wise listens to counsel. A fool shows his annoyance the same day, but one who overlooks an insult is prudent.

Proverbs 12:18 There is one who speaks rashly like the piercing of a sword, but the tongue of the wise heals.

Proverbs 12:25 Anxiety in a man's heart weighs it down, but a kind word makes it glad.

Proverbs 13:3 He who guards his mouth guards his soul. One who opens wide his lips comes to ruin.

Proverbs 13:12 Hope deferred makes the heart sick, but when longing is fulfilled, it is a tree of life.

Proverbs 13:17 A wicked messenger falls into trouble, but a trustworthy envoy gains healing.

Proverbs 14:12 There is a way which seems right to a man, but in the end it leads to death.

Proverbs 14:30 The life of the body is a heart at peace, but envy rots the bones.

Proverbs 15:3 Yahweh's eyes are everywhere, keeping watch on the evil and the good.

Proverbs 15:4 A gentle tongue is a tree of life, but deceit in it crushes the spirit.

Proverbs 15:13 A glad heart makes a cheerful face, but an aching heart breaks the spirit.

Proverbs 15:15 All the days of the afflicted are wretched, but one who has a cheerful heart enjoys a continual feast.

Proverbs 15:30 The light of the eyes rejoices the heart. Good news gives health to the bones.

Proverbs 15:31 The ear that listens to reproof lives, and will be at home among the wise.

Proverbs 16:2 All the ways of a man are clean in his own eyes; but Yahweh weighs the motives.

Proverbs 16:3 Commit your deeds to Yahweh, and your plans shall succeed.

Proverbs 16:18 Pride goes before destruction, and an arrogant spirit before a fall.

Proverbs 16:20 He who heeds the Word finds prosperity. Whoever trusts in Yahweh is blessed.

Proverbs 16:24 Pleasant words are a honeycomb, sweet to the soul, and health to the bones.

Proverbs 17:1 Better is a dry morsel with quietness, than a house full of feasting with strife.

Proverbs 17:22 A cheerful heart makes good medicine, but a crushed spirit dries up the bones.

Proverbs 18:8 The words of a gossip are like dainty morsels: they go down into a person's innermost parts.

Proverbs 18:14 A man's spirit will sustain him in sickness, but a crushed spirit, who can bear?

Proverbs 18:20 A man's stomach is filled with the fruit of his mouth. With the harvest of his lips he is satisfied.

Proverbs 18:21 Death and life are in the power of the tongue; those who love it will eat its fruit.

Proverbs 19:15 Slothfulness casts into a deep sleep. The idle soul shall suffer hunger.

Proverbs 20:1 Wine is a mocker and beer is a brawler. Whoever is led astray by them is not wise.

Proverbs 21:21 He who follows after righteousness and kindness finds life, righteousness, and honor.

Proverbs 21:31 The horse is prepared for the day of battle; but victory is with Yahweh.

Proverbs 22:11 He who loves purity of heart and speaks gracefully is the king's friend.

Proverbs 23:6-7 Don't eat the food of him who has a stingy eye, and don't crave his delicacies: for as he thinks about the cost, so he is. "Eat and drink!" he says to you, but his heart is not with you.

Proverbs 23:21 ...for the drunkard and the glutton shall become poor; and drowsiness clothes them in rags.

Proverbs 23:26 My son, give me your heart; and let your eyes keep in my ways.

Proverbs 23:29-30 Who has woe? Who has sorrow? Who has strife? Who has complaints? Who has needless bruises? Who has bloodshot eyes? Those who stay long at the wine; those who go to seek out mixed wine.

Proverbs 24:10-12 If you falter in the time of trouble, your strength is small. Rescue those who are being led away to death! Indeed, hold back those who are staggering to the slaughter!

Proverbs 24:13-14 My son, eat honey, for it is good, the droppings of the honeycomb, which are sweet to your taste; so you shall know wisdom to be to your soul. If you have found it, then there will be a reward: Your hope will not be cut off.

Proverbs 24:16-18 ...for a righteous man falls seven times and rises up again; but the wicked are overthrown by calamity. Don't rejoice when your enemy falls. Don't let your heart be glad when he is overthrown, lest Yahweh see it, and it displease him, and he turn away his wrath from him.

Proverbs 25:15 By patience a ruler is persuaded. A soft tongue breaks the bone.

Proverbs 25:19 Confidence in someone unfaithful in time of trouble is like a bad tooth or a lame foot.

Proverbs 25:23 The north wind produces rain; so a backbiting tongue brings an angry face.

Proverbs 26:2 Like a fluttering sparrow, like a darting swallow, so the undeserved curse doesn't come to rest.

Proverbs 26:6-7 One who sends a message by the hand of a fool is cutting off feet and drinking violence. Like the legs of the lame that hang loose, so is a parable in the mouth of fools.

Proverbs 26:8-9 As one who binds a stone in a sling, so is he who gives honor to a fool. Like a thorn bush that goes into the hand of a drunkard, so is a parable in the mouth of fools.

Proverbs 29:22-25 An angry man stirs up strife, and a wrathful man abounds in sin. A man's pride brings him low, but one of lowly spirit gains honor. Whoever is an accomplice of a thief is an enemy of his own soul. He takes an oath, but dares not testify. The fear of man proves to be a snare, but whoever puts his trust in Yahweh is kept safe.

Proverbs 30:14 There is a generation whose teeth are like swords, and their jaws like knives, to devour the poor from the earth, and the needy from among men.

Proverbs 30:17 "The eye that mocks at his father, and scorns obedience to his mother: the ravens of the valley shall pick it out, the young eagles shall eat it."

Ecclesiastes 3:1-2 For everything there is a season, and a time for every purpose under heaven: a time to be born, and a time to die; a time to plant, and a time to pluck up that which is planted;

Ecclesiastes 3:3 ...a time to kill, and a time to heal; a time to break down, and a time to build up;

Ecclesiastes 3:6 ...a time to seek, and a time to lose; a time to keep, and a time to cast away;

Ecclesiastes 5:12 The sleep of a laboring man is sweet, whether he eats little or much; but the abundance of the rich will not allow him to sleep.

Ecclesiastes 6:1-2 There is an evil which I have seen under the sun, and it is heavy on men: a man to whom God gives riches, wealth, and honor, so that he lacks nothing for his soul of all that he desires, yet God gives him no power to eat of it, but an alien eats it. This is vanity, and it is an evil disease.

Ecclesiastes 9:17-18 The words of the wise heard in quiet are better than the cry of him who rules among fools. Wisdom is better than weapons of war; but one sinner destroys much good.

Isaiah 1:4-6 Ah sinful nation, a people loaded with iniquity, offspring of evildoers, children who deal corruptly! They have forsaken Yahweh. They have despised the Holy One of Israel. They are estranged and backward. Why should you be beaten more, that you revolt more and more? The whole head is sick, and the whole heart faint. From the sole of the foot even to the head there is no soundness in it: wounds, welts, and open sores.

They haven't been closed, bandaged, or soothed with oil.

Isaiah 5:21 Woe to those who are wise in their own eyes, and prudent in their own sight!

Isaiah 6:9-10 He said, "Go, and tell this people, 'You hear indeed, but don't understand. You see indeed, but don't perceive.' Make the heart of this people fat. Make their ears heavy, and shut their eyes; lest they see with their eyes, hear with their ears, understand with their heart, and turn again, and be healed."

Isaiah 8:19-20 When they tell you, "Consult with those who have familiar spirits and with the wizards, who chirp and who mutter," shouldn't a people consult with their God? Should they consult the dead on behalf of the living? Turn to the law and to the covenant! If they don't speak according to this word, surely there is no morning for them.

Isaiah 10:27 It will happen in that day that his burden will depart from off your shoulder, and his yoke from off your neck, and the yoke shall be destroyed because of the anointing oil.

Isaiah 12:2-3 Behold, God is my salvation. I will trust, and will not be afraid; for Yah, Yahweh, is my strength and song; and he has become my salvation." Therefore with joy you will draw water out of the wells of salvation.

Isaiah 13:7-8 Therefore all hands will be feeble, and everyone's heart will melt. They will be dismayed. Pangs and sorrows will seize them. They will be in pain like a woman in labor. They will look in amazement one at another. Their faces will be faces of flame.

Isaiah 14:24-25 Yahweh of Armies has sworn, saying, "Surely, as I have thought, so shall it happen; and as I have purposed, so shall it stand: that I will break the Assyrian in my land, and tread him under foot on my mountains. Then his yoke will leave them, and his burden leave their shoulders."

Isaiah 19:22 Yahweh will strike Egypt, striking and healing. They will return to Yahweh, and he will be entreated by them, and will heal them.

Isaiah 30:26 Moreover the light of the moon will be like the light of the sun, and the light of the sun will be seven times brighter, like the light of seven days, in the day that Yahweh binds up the fracture of his people, and heals the wound they were struck with.

Isaiah 32:3 The eyes of those who see will not be dim, and the ears of those who hear will listen.

Isaiah 32:4 The heart of the rash will understand knowledge, and the tongue of the stammerers will be ready to speak plainly.

Isaiah 32:18 My people will live in a peaceful habitation, in safe dwellings, and in quiet resting places,

Isaiah 35:3 Strengthen the weak hands, and make the feeble knees firm.

Isaiah 35:4-5 Tell those who have a fearful heart, "Be strong! Don't be afraid! Behold, your God will come with vengeance, God's retribution. He will come and save you. Then the eyes of the blind will be opened, and the ears of the deaf will be unstopped."

Isaiah 35:6 Then the lame man will leap like a deer, and the tongue of the mute will sing; for waters will break out in the wilderness, and streams in the desert.

Isaiah 35:10 "Then Yahweh's ransomed ones will return, and come with singing to Zion; and everlasting joy will be on their heads. They will obtain gladness and joy, and sorrow and sighing will flee away."

Isaiah 38:5-6 "Go, and tell Hezekiah, 'Yahweh, the God of David your father, says, "I have heard your prayer. I have seen your tears. Behold, I will add fifteen years to your life. I will deliver you and this city out of the hand of the king of Assyria, and I will defend this city."'"

Isaiah 38:13-14 "I waited patiently until morning. He breaks all my bones like a lion. From day even to night you will make an end of me. I chattered like a swallow or a crane. I moaned like a dove. My eyes weaken looking upward. Lord, I am oppressed. Be my security."

Isaiah 38:16-17 Lord, men live by these things; and my spirit finds life in all of them: you restore me, and cause me to live. Behold, for peace I had great anguish, but you have in love for my soul delivered it from the pit of corruption; for you have cast all my sins behind your back.

Isaiah 40:29 He gives power to the weak. He increases the strength of him who has no might.

Isaiah 40:31 ...but those who wait for Yahweh will renew their strength. They will mount up with wings like eagles. They will run, and not be weary. They will walk, and not faint.

Isaiah 41:10 Don't you be afraid, for I am with you. Don't be dismayed, for I am your God. I will strengthen you. Yes, I will help you. Yes,

I will uphold you with the right hand of my righteousness.

Isaiah 41:13 "For I, Yahweh your God, will hold your right hand, saying to you, 'Don't be afraid. I will help you.'"

Isaiah 42:16 "I will bring the blind by a way that they don't know. I will lead them in paths that they don't know. I will make darkness light before them, and crooked places straight. I will do these things, and I will not forsake them."

Isaiah 43:1-3 But now Yahweh who created you, Jacob, and he who formed you, Israel, says: "Don't be afraid, for I have redeemed you. I have called you by your name. You are mine. When you pass through the waters, I will be with you, and through the rivers, they will not overflow you. When you walk through the fire, you will not be burned, and flame will not scorch you. For I am Yahweh your God, the Holy One of Israel, your Savior. I have given Egypt as your ransom, Ethiopia and Seba in your place."

Isaiah 43:25-26 "I, even I, am he who blots out your transgressions for my own sake; and I will not remember your sins. Put me in remembrance. Let us plead together. Declare your case, that you may be justified."

Isaiah 44:20 He feeds on ashes. A deceived heart has turned him aside; and he can't deliver his soul, nor say, "Isn't there a lie in my right hand?"

Isaiah 46:4 "Even to old age I am he, and even to gray hairs I will carry you. I have made, and I will bear. Yes, I will carry, and will deliver."

Isaiah 53:4 Surely he has borne our sickness and carried our suffering; yet we considered him plagued, struck by God, and afflicted.

Isaiah 53:5 But he was pierced for our transgressions. He was crushed for our iniquities. The punishment that brought our peace was on him; and by his wounds we are healed.

Isaiah 53:6 All we like sheep have gone astray. Everyone has turned to his own way; and Yahweh has laid on him the iniquity of us all.

Isaiah 53:10 Yet it pleased Yahweh to bruise him. He has caused him to suffer. When you make his soul an offering for sin, he will see his offspring. He will prolong his days and Yahweh's pleasure will prosper in his hand.

Isaiah 54:1 "Sing, barren, you who didn't give birth; break out into singing, and cry aloud, you who didn't travail with child: or more are the children of the desolate than the children of the married wife," says Yahweh.

Isaiah 54:4 "Don't be afraid, for you will not be ashamed. Don't be confounded, for you will not be disappointed. For you will forget the shame of your youth. You will remember the reproach of your widowhood no more."

Isaiah 54:13 "All your children will be taught by Yahweh; and your children's peace will be great."

Isaiah 54:14   "You will be established in righteousness. You will be far from oppression, for you will not be afraid, and far from terror, for it shall not come near you."

Isaiah 55:11 "...so is my word that goes out of my mouth: it will not return to me void, but it will accomplish that which I please, and it will prosper in the thing I sent it to do."

Isaiah 57:18 "I have seen his ways, and will heal him. I will lead him also, and restore comforts to him and to his mourners."

Isaiah 57:19 "I create the fruit of the lips: Peace, peace, to him who is far off and to him who is near," says Yahweh; "and I will heal them."

Isaiah 58:8 Then your light will break out as the morning, and your healing will appear quickly; then your righteousness shall go before you, and Yahweh's glory will be your rear guard.

Isaiah 58:10 ...and if you pour out your soul to the hungry, and satisfy the afflicted soul, then your light will rise in darkness, and your obscurity will be as the noonday;

Isaiah 59:21 "As for me, this is my covenant with them," says Yahweh. "My Spirit who is on you, and my words which I have put in your mouth shall not depart out of your mouth, nor out of the mouth of your offspring, nor out of the mouth of your offspring's offspring," says Yahweh, "from now on and forever."

Isaiah 61:1-3 The Lord Yahweh's Spirit is on me, because Yahweh has anointed me to preach good news to the humble. He has sent me to bind up the broken hearted, to proclaim liberty to the captives and release to those who are bound, to proclaim the year of Yahweh's favor and the day of vengeance of our God, to comfort all who mourn, to provide for those who mourn in Zion, to give to them a garland for ashes, the oil of joy for mourning, the garment of praise for the spirit of heaviness, that they may be called trees of righteousness, the planting of Yahweh, that he may be glorified.

Jeremiah 1:5 "Before I formed you in the womb, I knew you. Before you were born, I sanctified you. I have appointed you a prophet to the nations."

Jeremiah 1:12 Then Yahweh said to me, "You have seen well; for I watch over my word to perform it."

Jeremiah 3:22 Return, you backsliding children, and I will heal your backsliding. "Behold, we have come to you; for you are Yahweh our God."

Jeremiah 15:18-19 Why is my pain perpetual, and my wound incurable, which refuses to be healed? Will you indeed be to me as a deceitful brook, like waters that fail? Therefore Yahweh says, "If you return, then I will bring you again, that you may stand before me; and if you take out the precious from the vile, you will be as my mouth. They will return to you, but you will not return to them."

Jeremiah 16:19 Yahweh, my strength, and my stronghold, and my refuge in the day of affliction, the nations will come to you from the ends of the earth, and will say, "Our fathers have inherited nothing but lies, vanity and things in which there is no profit."

Jeremiah 17:5   Yahweh says: "Cursed is the man who trusts in man, relies on strength of flesh, and whose heart departs from Yahweh."

Jeremiah 17:7   Blessed is the man who trusts in Yahweh, and whose confidence is in Yahweh.

Jeremiah 17:9-10   The heart is deceitful above all things and it is exceedingly corrupt. Who can know it? "I, Yahweh, search the mind. I try the heart, even to give every man according to his ways, according to the fruit of his doings."

Jeremiah 17:14   Heal me, O Yahweh, and I will be healed. Save me, and I will be saved; for you are my praise.

Jeremiah 29:11   "For I know the thoughts that I think toward you," says Yahweh, "thoughts of peace, and not of evil, to give you hope and a future."

Jeremiah 30:15 Why do you cry over your injury? Your pain is incurable. For the greatness of your iniquity, because your sins have increased, I have done these things to you.

Jeremiah 30:17 "For I will restore health to you, and I will heal you of your wounds," says Yahweh; "because they have called you an outcast, saying, 'It is Zion, whom no man seeks after.'"

Jeremiah 31:13 "Then the virgin will rejoice in the dance; the young men and the old together; for I will turn their mourning into joy, and will comfort them, and make them rejoice from their sorrow."

Jeremiah 31:24-26 "Judah and all its cities will dwell therein together, the farmers, and those who go about with flocks. For I have satiated the weary soul, and I have replenished every sorrowful soul." On this I awakened, and saw; and my sleep was sweet to me.

Jeremiah 33:6 "Behold, I will bring it health and cure, and I will cure them; and I will reveal to them abundance of peace and truth."

Lamentations 1:3 Judah has gone into captivity because of affliction, and because of great servitude. She dwells among the nations. She finds no rest. All her persecutors overtook her within the straits.

Lamentations 1:9 Her filthiness was in her skirts. She didn't remember her latter end. Therefore she has come down astoundingly. She has no comforter. "See, Yahweh, my affliction; for the enemy has magnified himself."

Lamentations 1:13 "From on high has he sent fire into my bones, and it prevails against them. He has spread a net for my feet. He has turned me back. He has made me desolate and I faint all day long."

Lamentation 3:22-24 It is because of Yahweh's loving kindnesses that we are not consumed, because his compassion doesn't fail. They are new every morning. Great is your faithfulness. "Yahweh is my portion," says my soul. "Therefore I will hope in him."

Lamentations 5:12-14 Princes were hanged up by their hands. The faces of elders were not honored. The young men carry millstones. The children stumbled under loads of wood. The elders have ceased from the gate, and the young men from their music.

Ezekiel 3:3 He said to me, "Son of man, cause your belly to eat, and fill your bowels with this scroll that I give you." Then I ate it; and it was as sweet as honey in my mouth.

Ezekiel 6:9-10 "Those of you that escape will remember me among the nations where they are carried captive, how I have been broken with their lewd heart, which has departed from me, and with their eyes, which play the prostitute after their idols. Then they will loathe themselves in their own sight for the evils which they have committed in all their abominations. They will know that I am Yahweh. I have not said in vain that I would do this evil to them."

Ezekiel 7:15-18 "The sword is outside, and the pestilence and the famine within. He who is in the field will die by the sword. He who is in the city will be devoured by famine and pestilence. But those of those who escape, they will escape and will be on the mountains like doves of the valleys, all of them moaning, everyone in his iniquity. All hands will be feeble, and all knees will be weak as water. They will also clothe themselves with sackcloth, and horror will cover them. Shame will be on all faces, and baldness on all their heads."

Ezekiel 34:16 "I will seek that which was lost, and will bring back that which was driven away, and will bind up that which was broken, and will strengthen that which was sick; but I will destroy the fat and the strong. I will feed them in justice."

Ezekiel 36:26 "I will also give you a new heart, and I will put a new spirit within you. I will take away the stony heart out of your flesh, and I will give you a heart of flesh."

Ezekiel 37:5 The Lord Yahweh says to these bones: "Behold, I will cause breath to enter into you, and you will live."

Ezekiel 37:6 "I will lay sinews on you, and will bring up flesh on you, and cover you with skin, and put breath in you, and you will live. Then you will know that I am Yahweh."

Ezekiel 37:9 Then he said to me, "Prophesy to the wind, prophesy, son of man, and tell the wind, 'The Lord Yahweh says: "Come from the four winds, on breath, and breathe these slain, that they may live."'"

Ezekiel 37:11-12 Then he said to me, "Son of man, these bones are the whole house of Israel. Behold, they say, 'Our bones are dried up, and our hope is lost. We are completely cut off.' Therefore prophesy, and tell them, 'The Lord Yahweh says: "Behold, I will open your graves, and cause you to come up out of your graves, my people; and I will bring you into the land of Israel."'"

Ezekiel 37:14 "I will put my Spirit in you, and you will live. Then I will place you in your own land; and you will know that I, Yahweh, have spoken it and performed it," says Yahweh.

Ezekiel 47:9 "It will happen, that every living creature which swarms, in every place where the rivers come, will live. Then there will be a very great multitude of fish; for these waters have come there, and the waters of the sea will be healed, and everything will live wherever the river comes."

Ezekiel 47:12 "By the river on its bank, on this side and on that side, will grow every tree for food, whose leaf won't wither, neither will its fruit fail. It will produce new fruit every month, because its waters issue out of the sanctuary. Its fruit will be for food, and its leaf for healing."

Daniel 2:1 In the second year of the reign of Nebuchadnezzar, Nebuchadnezzar dreamed dreams; and his spirit was troubled, and his sleep went from him.

Daniel 3:28 Nebuchadnezzar spoke and said, "Blessed be the God of Shadrach, Meshach, and Abednego, who has sent his angel and delivered his servants who trusted in him, and have changed the king's word, and have yielded their bodies, that they might not serve nor worship any god, except their own God."

Daniel 9:8 Lord, to us belongs confusion of face, to our kings, to our princes, and to our fathers, because we have sinned against you.

Hosea 4:2-3 There is cursing, lying, murder, stealing, and committing adultery; they break boundaries, and bloodshed causes bloodshed. Therefore the land will mourn, and everyone who dwells in it will waste away, with all living things in her, even the animals of the field and the birds of the sky; yes, the fish of the sea also die.

Hosea 4:6 "My people are destroyed for lack of knowledge. Because you have rejected knowledge, I will also reject you, that you may be no priest to me. Because you have forgotten your God's law, I will also forget your children."

Hosea 6:1 "Come! Let's return to Yahweh; for he has torn us to pieces, and he will heal us; he has injured us, and he will bind up our wounds."

Hosea 11:3 "Yet I taught Ephraim to walk. I took them by his arms; but they didn't know that I healed them."

Hosea 13:12-13 "The guilt of Ephraim is stored up. His sin is stored up. The sorrows of a travailing woman will come on him. He is an unwise son; for when it is time, he doesn't come to the opening of the womb."

Hosea 13:14 "I will ransom them from the power of Sheol. I will redeem them from death! Death, where are your plagues? Sheol, where is your destruction? 'Compassion will be hidden from my eyes.'"

Hosea 14:4 "I will heal their waywardness. I will love them freely; for my anger is turned away from him."

Joel 2:28 "It will happen afterward, that I will pour out my Spirit on all flesh; and your sons and your daughters will prophesy. Your old men will dream dreams. Your young men will see visions."

Joel 3:10 "Beat your plowshares into swords, and your pruning hooks into spears. Let the weak say, 'I am strong.'"

Amos 5:4 For Yahweh says to the house of Israel: "Seek me, and you will live."

Micah 4:6-7 "In that day," says Yahweh, "I will assemble that which is lame, and I will gather that which is driven away, and that which I have afflicted; and I will make that which was lame a remnant, and that which was cast far off a strong nation: and Yahweh will reign over them on Mount Zion from then on, even forever."

Nahum 1:7-9 Yahweh is good, a stronghold in the day of trouble; and he knows those who take refuge in him. But with an overflowing flood, he will make a full end of her place, and will pursue his enemies into darkness. What do you plot against Yahweh? He will make a full end. Affliction won't rise up the second time.

Zechariah 4:1 The angel who talked with me came again, and wakened me, as a man who is wakened out of his sleep.

Malachi 3:10 "Bring the whole tithe into the storehouse, that there may be food in my house, and test me now in this," says Yahweh of Armies, "if I will not open you the windows of heaven, and pour you out a blessing, that there will not be room enough for."

Malachi 3:11 "I will rebuke the devourer for your sakes, and he shall not destroy the fruits of your ground; neither shall your vine cast its fruit before its time in the field," says Yahweh of Armies.

Malachi 4:2 "But to you who fear my name shall the sun of righteousness arise with healing in its wings. You will go out, and leap like calves of the stall."

New Testament Scriptures

Matthew 4:4 But he answered, "It is written, 'Man shall not live by bread alone, but by every word that proceeds out of God's mouth.'"

Matthew 4:23 Jesus went about in all Galilee, teaching in their synagogues, preaching the Good News of the Kingdom, and healing every disease and every sickness among the people.

Matthew 4:24 The report about him went out into all Syria. They brought to him all who were sick, afflicted with various diseases and torments, possessed with demons, epileptics, and paralytics; and he healed them.

Matthew 6:10 "Let your Kingdom come. Let your will be done on earth as it is in heaven."

Matthew 6:13 "Bring us not into temptation, but deliver us from the evil one. For yours is the Kingdom, the power, and the glory forever. Amen."

Matthew 6:14-15 "For if you forgive men their trespasses, your heavenly Father will also forgive you. But if you don't forgive men their trespasses, neither will your Father forgive your trespasses."

Matthew 6:22-23 "The lamp of the body is the eye. If therefore your eye is sound, your whole body will be full of light. But if your eye is evil, your whole body will be full of darkness. If therefore the light that is in you is darkness, how great is the darkness!"

Matthew 6:25 "Therefore I tell you, don't be anxious for your life: what you will eat, or what you will drink; nor yet for your body, what you will wear. Isn't life more than food, and the body more than clothing?"

Matthew 6:34 "Therefore don't be anxious for tomorrow, for tomorrow will be anxious for itself. Each day's own evil is sufficient."

Matthew 7:1-4 "Don't judge, so that you won't be judged. For with whatever judgment you judge, you will be judged; and with whatever measure you measure, it will be measured to you. Why do you see the speck that is in your brother's eye, but don't consider the beam that is in your own eye? Or how will you tell your brother, 'Let me remove the speck from your eye,' and behold, the beam is in your own eye?'"

Matthew 7:7-9 "Ask, and it will be given you. Seek, and you will find. Knock, and it will be opened for you. To him who knocks it will be opened. Or who is there among you who, if his son asks him for bread, will give him a stone?"

Matthew 7:10-12 "Or if he asks for a fish, who will give him a serpent? If you then, being evil, know how to give good gifts to your children, how much more will your Father who is in heaven give good things to those who ask him! Therefore, whatever you desire for men to do to you, you shall also do to them; for this is the law and the prophets."

Matthew 8:2-3 Behold, a leper came to him and worshiped him, saying, "Lord, if you want to, you can make me clean." Jesus stretched out his hand and touched him, saying, "I want to. Be made clean." Immediately his leprosy was cleansed.

Matthew 8:7 Jesus said to him, "I will come and heal him."

Matthew 8:8 The centurion answered, "Lord, I'm not worthy for you to come under my roof. Just say the word, and my servant will be healed."

Matthew 8:9-10 For I am also a man under authority, having under myself soldiers. I tell this one, 'Go,' and he goes; and tell another, 'Come,' and he comes; and tell my servant, 'Do this,' and he does it." When Jesus heard it, he marveled and said to those who followed, "Most certainly I tell you, I haven't found so great a faith, not even in Israel."

Matthew 8:13 Jesus said to the centurion, "Go your way. Let it be done for you as you have believed." His servant was healed in that hour.

Matthew 8:15-16 He touched her hand, and the fever left her. So she got up and served him. When evening came, they brought to him many possessed with demons. He cast out the spirits with a word, and healed all who were sick,

Matthew 8:17 ...that it might be fulfilled which was spoken through Isaiah the prophet, saying, "He took our infirmities and bore our diseases."

Matthew 8:26 He said to them, "Why are you fearful, O you of little faith?" Then he got up, rebuked the wind and the sea, and there was a great calm.

Matthew 9:2 Behold, they brought to him a man who was paralyzed, lying on a bed. Jesus, seeing their faith, said to the paralytic, "Son, cheer up! Your sins are forgiven you."

Matthew 9:6-7 But that you may know that the Son of Man has authority on earth to forgive sins—" (then he said to the paralytic), "Get up, and take up your mat, and go to your house."

Matthew 9:12 When Jesus heard it, he said to them, "Those who are healthy have no need for a physician, but those who are sick do."

Matthew 9:21 ...for she said within herself, "If I just touch his garment, I will be made well."

Matthew 9:22 But Jesus, turning around and seeing her, said, "Daughter, cheer up! Your faith has made you well." And the woman was made well from that hour.

Matthew 9:28-30 When he had come into the house, the blind men came to him. Jesus said to them, "Do you believe that I am able to do this?" They told him, "Yes, Lord." Then he touched their eyes, saying, "According to your faith be it done to you." Then their eyes were opened. Jesus strictly commanded them, saying, "See that no one knows about this."

Matthew 9:32-33 As they went out, behold, a mute man who was demon possessed was brought to him. When the demon was cast out, the mute man spoke. The multitudes marveled, saying, "Nothing like this has ever been seen in Israel!"

Matthew 9:35 Jesus went about all the cities and the villages, teaching in their synagogues and preaching the Good News of the Kingdom, and healing every disease and every sickness among the people.

Matthew 10:1 He called to himself his twelve disciples, and gave them authority over unclean spirits, to cast them out, and to heal every disease and every sickness.

Matthew 10:8 Heal the sick, cleanse the lepers, and cast out demons. Freely you received, so freely give.

Matthew 10:30-31 "But the very hairs of your head are all numbered. Therefore don't be afraid. You are of more value than many sparrows."

Matthew 11:28-30 "Come to me, all you who labor and are heavily burdened, and I will give you rest. Take my yoke upon you and learn from me, for I am gentle and humble in heart; and you will find rest for your souls. For my yoke is easy, and my burden is light."

Matthew 12:10-13 And behold, there was a man with a withered hand. They asked him, "Is it lawful to heal on the Sabbath day?" so that they might accuse him. He said to them, "What man is there among you who has one sheep, and if this one falls into a pit on the Sabbath day, won't he grab on to it and lift it out? Of how much more value then is a man than a sheep! Therefore it is lawful to do good on the Sabbath day." Then he told the man, "Stretch out your hand." He stretched it out; and it was restored whole, just like the other.

Matthew 12:15 Jesus, perceiving that, withdrew from there. Great multitudes followed him; and he healed them all,

Matthew 12:22 Then one possessed by a demon, blind and mute, was brought to him; and he healed him, so that the blind and mute man both spoke and saw.

Matthew 13:15 "...for this people's heart has grown callous, their ears are dull of hearing, and they have closed their eyes; or else perhaps they might perceive with their eyes, hear with their ears, understand with their heart, and would turn again, and I would heal them."

Matthew 13:16 "But blessed are your eyes, for they see; and your ears, for they hear."

Matthew 13:49-50 "So will it be in the end of the world. The angels will come and separate the wicked from among the righteous, and will cast them into the furnace of fire. There will be weeping and gnashing of teeth."

Matthew 13:58 He didn't do many mighty works there because of their unbelief.

Matthew 14:14 Jesus went out, and he saw a great multitude. He had compassion on them and healed their sick.

Matthew 14:35-36 When the people of that place recognized him, they sent into all that surrounding region and brought to him all who were sick; and they begged him that they might just touch the fringe of his garment. As many as touched it were made whole.

Matthew 15:25-28 But she came and worshiped him, saying, "Lord, help me." But he answered, "It is not appropriate to take the children's bread and throw it to the dogs." But she said, "Yes, Lord, but even the dogs eat the crumbs which fall from their masters' table." Then Jesus answered her, "Woman, great is your faith! Be it done to you even as you desire." And her daughter was healed from that hour.

Matthew 15:29-31 Jesus departed from there and came near to the sea of Galilee; and he went up into the mountain and sat there. Great multitudes came to him, having with them the lame, blind, mute, maimed, and many others, and they put them down at his feet. He healed them, so that the multitude wondered when they saw the mute speaking, the injured healed, the lame walking, and the blind seeing—and they glorified the God of Israel.

Matthew 16:23 But he turned and said to Peter, "Get behind me, Satan! You are a stumbling block to me, for you are not setting your mind on the things of God, but on the things of men."

Matthew 16:28 "Most certainly I tell you, there are some standing here who will in no way taste of death until they see the Son of Man coming in his Kingdom."

Matthew 17:15, 18 "Lord, have mercy on my son, for he is epileptic and suffers grievously; for he often falls into the fire, and often into the water." Jesus rebuked the demon, and it went out of him, and the boy was cured from that hour. Whatever you bind on earth will have been bound in heaven, and whatever things you release on earth will have been released in heaven.

Matthew 18:6-7 ...but whoever causes one of these little ones who believe in me to stumble, it would be better for him if a huge millstone were hung around his neck and that he were sunk in the depths of the sea. "Woe to the world because of occasions of stumbling! For it must be that the occasions come, but woe to that person through whom the occasion comes!"

Matthew 18:18 Most certainly I tell you, whatever things you bind on earth will have been bound in heaven, and whatever things you release on earth will have been released in heaven.

Matthew 18:19 "Again, assuredly I tell you, that if two of you will agree on earth concerning anything that they will ask, it will be done for them by my Father who is in heaven."

Matthew 18:34 His lord was angry, and delivered him to the tormentors until he should pay all that was due to him.

Matthew 19:2 Great multitudes followed him, and he healed them there.

Matthew 20:30, 32-34 Behold, two blind men sitting by the road, when they heard that Jesus was passing by, cried out, "Lord, have mercy on us, you son of David!" Jesus stood still and called them, and asked, "What do you want me to do for you?" They told him, "Lord, that our eyes may be opened." Jesus, being moved with compassion, touched their eyes; and immediately their eyes received their sight, and they followed him.

Matthew 21:14 The lame and the blind came to him in the temple, and he healed them.

Matthew 21:21 Jesus answered them, "Most certainly I tell you, if you have faith and don't doubt, you will not only do what was done to the fig tree, but even if you told this mountain, 'Be taken up and cast into the sea,' it would be done."

Matthew 22:37-40 Jesus said to him, "'You shall love the Lord your God with all your heart, with all your soul, and with all your mind. This is the first and great commandment. A second likewise is this, 'You shall love your neighbor as yourself.' The whole law and the prophets depend on these two commandments."

Matthew 25:36 "I was naked and you clothed me. I was sick and you visited me. I was in prison and you came to me."

Matthew 26:27-28 He took the cup, gave thanks, and gave to them, saying, "All of you drink it, for this is my blood of the new covenant, which is poured out for many for the remission of sins."

Matthew 26:41 "Watch and pray, that you don't enter into temptation. The spirit indeed is willing, but the flesh is weak."

Mark 1:31 He came and took her by the hand and raised her up. The fever left her immediately, and she served them.

Mark 1:34 He healed many who were sick with various diseases and cast out many demons. He didn't allow the demons to speak, because they knew him.

Mark 1:40-42 A leper came to him, begging him, kneeling down to him, and saying to him, "If you want to, you can make me clean." Being moved with compassion, he stretched out his hand, and touched him, and said to him, "I want to. Be made clean." When he had said this, immediately the leprosy departed from him and he was made clean.

Mark 2:3-5 Four people came, carrying a paralytic to him. When they could not come near to him for the crowd, they removed the roof where he was. When they had broken it up, they let down the mat that the paralytic was lying on. Jesus, seeing their faith, said to the paralytic, "Son, your sins are forgiven you."

Mark 2:17 When Jesus heard it, he said to them, "Those who are healthy have no need for a physician, but those who are sick. I came not to call the righteous, but sinners to repentance."

Mark 3:5 When he had looked around at them with anger, being grieved at the hardening of their hearts, he said to the man, "Stretch out your hand." He stretched it out, and his hand was restored as healthy as the other.

Mark 3:10 For he had healed many, so that as many as had diseases pressed on him that they might touch him.

Mark 5:29 Immediately the flow of her blood was dried up, and she felt in her body that she was healed of her affliction.

Mark 5:36 But Jesus, when he heard the message spoken, immediately said to the ruler of the synagogue, "Don't be afraid, only believe."

Mark 6:4-5 Jesus said to them, "A prophet is not without honor, except in his own country, and among his own relatives, and in his own house." He could do no mighty work there, except that he laid his hands on a few sick people, and healed them.

Mark 6:13 They cast out many demons, and anointed many with oil who were sick, and healed them.

Mark 6:56 Wherever he entered, into villages, or into cities, or into the country, they laid the sick in the marketplaces, and begged him that they might just touch the fringe of his garment; and as many as touched him were made well.

Mark 7:15 There is nothing from outside of the man, that going into him can defile him; but the things which proceed out of the man are those that defile the man.

Mark 7:33-35 He took him aside from the multitude, privately, and put his fingers into his ears, and he spat, and touched his tongue. Looking up to heaven, he sighed, and said to him, "Ephphatha!" that is, "Be opened!" Immediately his ears were opened, and the impediment of his tongue was released, and he spoke clearly.

Mark 7:37 They were astonished beyond measure, saying, "He has done all things well. He makes even the deaf hear, and the mute speak!"

Mark 8:25 Then again he laid his hands on his eyes. He looked intently, and was restored, and saw everyone clearly.

Mark 9:17 One of the multitude answered, "Teacher, I brought to you my son, who has a mute spirit;"

Mark 9:23-24 Jesus said to him, "If you can believe, all things are possible to him who believes." Immediately the father of the child cried out with tears, "I believe. Help my unbelief!"

Mark 9:25 When Jesus saw that a multitude came running together, he rebuked the unclean spirit, saying to him, "You mute and deaf spirit, I command you, come out of him, and never enter him again!"

Mark 10:52 Jesus said to him, "Go your way. Your faith has made you well." Immediately he received his sight, and followed Jesus on the way.

Mark 11:22-24 Jesus answered them, "Have faith in God. For most certainly I tell you, whoever may tell this mountain, 'Be taken up and cast into the sea,' and doesn't doubt in his heart, but believes that what he says is happening; he shall have whatever he says. Therefore I tell you, all things whatever you pray and ask for, believe that you have received them, and you shall have them."

Mark 12:29-31 Jesus answered, "The greatest is, 'Hear, Israel, the Lord our God, the Lord is one:

you shall love the Lord your God with all your heart, and with all your soul, and with all your mind, and with all your strength.' This is the first commandment. The second is like this, 'You shall love your neighbor as yourself.' There is no other commandment greater than these."

Mark 16:14 Afterward he was revealed to the eleven themselves as they sat at the table, and he rebuked them for their unbelief and hardness of heart, because they didn't believe those who had seen him after he had risen.

Mark 16:17-18 "These signs will accompany those who believe: in my name they will cast out demons; they will speak with new languages; they will take up serpents; and if they drink any deadly thing, it will in no way hurt them; they will lay hands on the sick, and they will recover."

Luke 1:36 Behold, Elizabeth your relative also has conceived a son in her old age; and this is the sixth month with her who was called barren.

Luke 4:18-19 "The Spirit of the Lord is on me, because he has anointed me to preach good news to the poor. He has sent me to heal the broken hearted, to proclaim release to the captives, recovering of sight to the blind, to deliver those who are crushed, and to proclaim the acceptable year of the Lord."

Luke 4:35-36 Jesus rebuked him, saying, "Be silent, and come out of him!" When the demon had thrown him down in the middle of them, he came out of him, having done him no harm.- Amazement came on all, and they spoke together, one with another, saying, "What is this word? For with authority and power he commands the unclean spirits, and they come out!"

Luke 4:39 He stood over her, and rebuked the fever; and it left her. Immediately she rose up and served them.

Luke 4:40 When the sun was setting, all those who had any sick with various diseases brought them to him; and he laid his hands on every one of them, and healed them.

Luke 5:12-13 While he was in one of the cities, behold, there was a man full of leprosy. When he saw Jesus, he fell on his face, and begged him, saying, "Lord, if you want to, you can make me clean." He stretched out his hand, and touched him, saying, "I want to. Be made clean." Immediately the leprosy left him.

Luke 5:15 But the report concerning him spread much more, and great multitudes came together to hear, and to be healed by him of their infirmities.

Luke 5:17 On one of those days, he was teaching; and there were Pharisees and teachers of the law sitting by, who had come out of every village of Galilee, Judea, and Jerusalem. The power of the Lord was with him to heal them.

Luke 5:31-32 Jesus answered them, "Those who are healthy have no need for a physician, but those who are sick do. I have not come to call the righteous, but sinners to repentance."

Luke 6:10 He looked around at them all, and said to the man, "Stretch out your hand." He did, and his hand was restored as sound as the other.

Luke 6:17 He came down with them, and stood on a level place, with a crowd of his disciples, and a great number of the people from all Judea and Jerusalem, and the sea coast of Tyre and Sidon, who came to hear him and to be healed of their diseases;

Luke 6:18 ...as well as those who were troubled by unclean spirits, and they were being healed.

Luke 6:19 All the multitude sought to touch him, for power came out of him and healed them all.

Luke 6:21 "Blessed are you who hunger now, for you will be filled. Blessed are you who weep now, for you will laugh."

Luke 7:7 Therefore I didn't even think myself worthy to come to you; but say the word, and my servant will be healed.

Luke 7:21 In that hour he cured many of diseases and plagues and evil spirits; and to many who were blind he gave sight.

Luke 7:22 Jesus answered them, "Go and tell John the things which you have seen and heard: that the blind receive their sight, the lame walk, the lepers are cleansed, the deaf hear, the dead are raised up, and the poor have good news preached to them."

Luke 8:2 ...and certain women who had been healed of evil spirits and infirmities: Mary who was called Magdalene, from whom seven demons had gone out;

Luke 8:29 For Jesus was commanding the unclean spirit to come out of the man. For the unclean spirit had often seized the man. He was kept under guard, and bound with chains and fetters. Breaking the bonds apart, he was driven by the demon into the desert.

Luke 8:36 Those who saw it told them how he who had been possessed by demons was healed.

Luke 8:47 When the woman saw that she was not hidden, she came trembling, and falling down before him declared to him in the presence of all the people the reason why she had touched him, and how she was healed immediately.

Luke 8:50 But Jesus hearing it, answered him, "Don't be afraid. Only believe, and she will be healed."

Luke 8:52-54 All were weeping and mourning her, but he said, "Don't weep. She isn't dead, but sleeping." They were ridiculing him, knowing that she was dead. But he put them all outside, and taking her by the hand, he called, saying, "Child, arise!"

Luke 9:1-2 He called the twelve together, and gave them power and authority over all demons, and to cure diseases. He sent them out to preach God's Kingdom and to heal the sick.

Luke 9:6 They departed and went throughout the villages, preaching the Good News and healing everywhere.

Luke 9:11 But the multitudes, perceiving it, followed him. He welcomed them, spoke to them of God's Kingdom, and he cured those who needed healing.

Luke 9:32 Now Peter and those who were with him were heavy with sleep, but when they were fully awake, they saw his glory, and the two men who stood with him.

Luke 9:56 "For the Son of Man didn't come to destroy men's lives, but to save them."

Luke 10:19 Behold, I give you authority to tread on serpents and scorpions, and over all the power of the enemy. Nothing will in any way hurt you.

Luke 10:33-34 But a certain Samaritan, as he traveled, came where he was. When he saw him, he was moved with compassion, came to him, and bound up his wounds, pouring on oil and wine. He set him on his own animal, brought him to an inn, and took care of him.

Luke 10:41-42 Jesus answered her, "Martha, Martha, you are anxious and troubled about many things, but one thing is needed. Mary has chosen the good part, which will not be taken away from her."

Luke 11:14 He was casting out a demon, and it was mute. When the demon had gone out, the mute man spoke; and the multitudes marveled.

Luke 11:20-23 But if I by God's finger cast out demons, then God's Kingdom has come to you. "When the strong man, fully armed, guards his own dwelling, his goods are safe. But when someone stronger attacks him and overcomes him, he takes from him his whole armor in which he trusted, and divides his plunder. "He that is not with me is against me. He who doesn't gather with me scatters."

Luke 11:24-26 "The unclean spirit, when he has gone out of the man, passes through dry places, seeking rest, and finding none, he says, 'I will turn back to my house from which I came out.' When he returns, he finds it swept and put in order. Then he goes, and takes seven other spirits more evil than himself, and they enter in and dwell there. The last state of that man becomes worse than the first."

Luke 13:11-13 Behold, there was a woman who had a spirit of infirmity eighteen years. She was bent over, and could in no way straighten herself up. When Jesus saw her, he called her, and said to her, "Woman, you are freed from your infirmity." He laid his hands on her, and immediately she stood up straight and glorified God.

Luke 14:2-4 Behold, a certain man who had dropsy was in front of him. Jesus, answering, spoke to the lawyers and Pharisees, saying, "Is it lawful to heal on the Sabbath?" But they were silent. He took him, and healed him, and let him go.

Luke 17:5-6 The apostles said to the Lord, "Increase our faith." The Lord said, "If you had faith like a grain of mustard seed, you would tell this sycamore tree, 'Be uprooted, and be planted in the sea,' and it would obey you."

Luke 17:15 One of them, when he saw that he was healed, turned back, glorifying God with a loud voice.

Luke 17:19 Then he said to him, "Get up, and go your way. Your faith has healed you."

Luke 18:42 Jesus said to him, "Receive your sight. Your faith has healed you."

John 1:4 In him was life, and the life was the light of men.

John 3:16 For God so loved the world, that he gave his one and only Son, that whoever believes in him should not perish, but have eternal life.

John 5:4 ...for an angel went down at certain times into the pool and stirred up the water. Whoever stepped in first after the stirring of the water was healed of whatever disease he had.

John 5:6 When Jesus saw him lying there, and knew that he had been sick for a long time, he asked him, "Do you want to be made well?"

John 5:8-9 Jesus said to him, "Arise, take up your mat, and walk." Immediately, the man was made well, and took up his mat and walked. Now it was the Sabbath on that day.

John 5:14 Afterward Jesus found him in the temple, and said to him, "Behold, you are made well. Sin no more, so that nothing worse happens to you."

John 5:24 "Most certainly I tell you, he who hears my word and believes him who sent me has eternal life, and doesn't come into judgment, but has passed out of death into life."

John 6:33-35 "For the bread of God is that which comes down out of heaven, and gives life to the world." They said therefore to him, "Lord, always give us this bread." Jesus said to them, "I am the bread of life. Whoever comes to me will not be hungry, and whoever believes in me will never be thirsty."

John 6:57 "As the living Father sent me, and I live because of the Father; so he who feeds on me, he will also live because of me."

John 6:58 "This is the bread which came down out of heaven—not as our fathers ate the manna, and died. He who eats this bread will live forever."

John 6:63 "It is the spirit who gives life. The flesh profits nothing. The words that I speak to you are spirit, and are life."

John 9:1-3 As he passed by, he saw a man blind from birth. His disciples asked him, "Rabbi, who sinned, this man or his parents, that he was born blind?" Jesus answered, "This man didn't sin, nor did his parents; but, that the works of God might be revealed in him."

John 9:31-32 We know that God doesn't listen to sinners, but if anyone is a worshiper of God, and does his will, he listens to him. Since the world began it has never been heard of that anyone opened the eyes of someone born blind.

John 10:10 "The thief only comes to steal, kill, and destroy. I came that they may have life, and may have it abundantly."

John 11:4 But when Jesus heard it, he said, "This sickness is not to death, but for the glory of God, that God's Son may be glorified by it."

John 11:10 "But if a man walks in the night, he stumbles, because the light isn't in him."

John 11:25 Jesus said to her, "I am the resurrection and the life. He who believes in me will still live, even if he dies."

John 11:42-44 "I know that you always listen to me, but because of the multitude standing around I said this, that they may believe that you sent me." When he had said this, he cried with a loud voice, "Lazarus, come out!" He who was dead came out, bound hand and foot with wrappings, and his face was wrapped around with a cloth. Jesus said to them, "Free him, and let him go."

John 14:1 "Don't let your heart be troubled. Believe in God. Believe also in me."

John 14:12-14 "Most certainly I tell you, he who believes in me, the works that I do, he will do also;

and he will do greater works than these, because I am going to my Father. Whatever you will ask in my name, I will do it, that the Father may be glorified in the Son. If you will ask anything in my name, I will do it."

John 14:15 "If you love me, keep my commandments."

John 14:21 "One who has my commandments and keeps them, that person is one who loves me. One who loves me will be loved by my Father, and I will love him, and will reveal myself to him."

John 14:27 "Peace I leave with you. My peace I give to you; not as the world gives, I give to you. Don't let your heart be troubled, neither let it be fearful."

John 15:7 "If you remain in me, and my words remain in you, you will ask whatever you desire, and it will be done for you."

John 15:11 "I have spoken these things to you, that my joy may remain in you, and that your joy may be made full."

John 16:33 "I have told you these things, that in me you may have peace. In the world you have trouble; but cheer up! I have overcome the world."

John 17:22 "The glory which you have given me, I have given to them; that they may be one, even as we are one;"

Acts 2:26 Therefore my heart was glad, and my tongue rejoiced. Moreover my flesh also will dwell in hope;

Acts 2:38 Peter said to them, "Repent, and be baptized, every one of you, in the name of Jesus Christ for the forgiveness of sins, and you will receive the gift of the Holy Spirit."

Acts 2:46 Day by day, continuing steadfastly with one accord in the temple, and breaking bread at home, they took their food with gladness and singleness of heart,

Acts 3:11 As the lame man who was healed held on to Peter and John, all the people ran together to them in the porch that is called Solomon's, greatly wondering.

Acts 3:16 By faith in his name, his name has made this man strong, whom you see and know. Yes, the faith which is through him has given him this perfect soundness in the presence of you all.

Acts 4:22 For the man on whom this miracle of healing was performed was more than forty years old.

Acts 4:30 "...while you stretch out your hand to heal; and that signs and wonders may be done through the name of your holy Servant Jesus."

Acts 5:16 The multitude also came together from the cities around Jerusalem, bringing sick people and those who were tormented by unclean spirits: and they were all healed.

Acts 5:19-20 But an angel of the Lord opened the prison doors by night, and brought them out and said, "Go stand and speak in the temple to the people all the words of this life."

Acts 9:12 ...and in a vision he has seen a man named Ananias coming in and laying his hands on him, that he might receive his sight.

Acts 9:18 Immediately something like scales fell from his eyes, and he received his sight. He arose and was baptized.

Acts 9:34 Peter said to him, "Aeneas, Jesus Christ heals you. Get up and make your bed!" Immediately he arose.

Acts 9:40 Peter sent them all out, and knelt down and prayed. Turning to the body, he said, "Tabitha, get up!" She opened her eyes, and when she saw Peter, she sat up.

Acts 10:38 ...even Jesus of Nazareth, how God anointed him with the Holy Spirit and with power, who went about doing good and healing all who were oppressed by the devil, for God was with him.

Acts 12:7 And behold, an angel of the Lord stood by him, and a light shone in the cell. He struck Peter on the side, and woke him up, saying, "Stand up quickly!" His chains fell off his hands.

Acts 12:23 Immediately an angel of the Lord struck him, because he didn't give God the glory. Then he was eaten by worms and died.

Acts 13:10-11 ...and said, "You son of the devil, full of all deceit and all cunning, you enemy of all righteousness, will you not cease to pervert the right ways of the Lord? Now, behold, the hand of the Lord is on you, and you will be blind, not seeing the sun for a season!" Immediately a mist and darkness fell on him. He went around seeking so.

Acts 14:8-10 At Lystra a certain man sat, impotent in his feet, a cripple from his mother's womb, who never had walked. He was listening to Paul speaking, who, fastening eyes on him, and seeing that he had faith to be made whole, said with a loud voice, "Stand upright on your feet!" He leaped up and walked.

Acts 16:26 Suddenly there was a great earthquake, so that the foundations of the prison were shaken; and immediately all the doors were opened, and everyone's bonds were loosened.

Acts 17:25 He isn't served by men's hands, as though he needed anything, seeing he himself gives to all life and breath, and all things.

Acts 19:12 ...so that even handkerchiefs or aprons were carried away from his body to the sick, and the diseases departed from them, and the evil spirits went out.

Acts 26:18 "...to open their eyes, that they may turn from darkness to light and from the power of Satan to God, that they may receive remission of sins and an inheritance among those who are sanctified by faith in me."

Acts 28:8-9 The father of Publius lay sick of fever and dysentery. Paul entered in to him, prayed, and laying his hands on him, healed him. Then when this was done, the rest also who had diseases in the island came and were cured.

Romans 1:24-25 Therefore God also gave them up in the lusts of their hearts to uncleanness, that their bodies should be dishonored among themselves; who exchanged the truth of God for a lie, and worshiped and served the creature rather than the Creator, who is blessed forever. Amen.

Romans 1:26-27 For this reason, God gave them up to vile passions. For their women changed the natural function into that which is against nature. Likewise also the men, leaving the natural function of the woman, burned in their lust toward one another, men doing what is inappropriate with men, and receiving in themselves the due penalty of their error.

Romans 2:1 Therefore you are without excuse, O man, whoever you are who judge. For in that which you judge another, you condemn yourself. For you who judge practice the same things.

Romans 3:4 May it never be! Yes, let God be found true, but every man a liar. As it is written, "that you might be justified in your words, and might prevail when you come into judgment..."

Romans 4:17 As it is written, "I have made you a father of many nations." This is in the presence of him whom he believed: God, who gives life to the dead, and calls the things that are not, as though they were.

Romans 4:19-21 Without being weakened in faith, he didn't consider his own body, already having been worn out, (he being about a hundred years old), and the deadness of Sarah's womb. Yet, looking to the promise of God, he didn't waver through unbelief, but grew strong through faith, giving glory to God, and being fully assured that what he had promised, he was also able to perform.

Romans 5:3-4   Not only this, but we also rejoice in our sufferings, knowing that suffering produces perseverance; and perseverance, proven character; and proven character, hope:

Romans 5:10   For if while we were enemies, we were reconciled to God through the death of his Son, much more, being reconciled, we will be saved by his life.

Romans 5:21   ...that as sin reigned in death, even so grace might reign through righteousness to eternal life through Jesus Christ our Lord.

Romans 6:4   We were buried therefore with him through baptism into death, that just as Christ was raised from the dead through the glory of the Father, so we also might walk in newness of life.

Romans 6:13 Also, do not present your members to sin as instruments of unrighteousness, but present yourselves to God as alive from the dead, and your members as instruments of righteousness to God.

Romans 6:16 Don't you know that when you present yourselves as servants and obey someone, you are the servants of whomever you obey; whether of sin to death, or of obedience to righteousness?

Romans 6:23 For the wages of sin is death, but the free gift of God is eternal life in Christ Jesus our Lord.

Romans 7:22-23 For I delight in God's law after the inward person, but I see a different law in my members, warring against the law of my mind, and bringing me into captivity under the law of sin which is in my members.

Romans 7:24-25 What a wretched man I am! Who will deliver me out of the body of this death? I thank God through Jesus Christ, our Lord! So then with the mind, I myself serve God's law, but with the flesh, sin's law.

Romans 8:1 There is therefore now no condemnation to those who are in Christ Jesus, who don't walk according to the flesh, but according to the Spirit.

Romans 8:2 For the law of the Spirit of life in Christ Jesus made me free from the law of sin and of death.

Romans 8:6 For the mind of the flesh is death, but the mind of the Spirit is life and peace;

Romans 8:9 But you are not in the flesh but in the Spirit, if it is so that the Spirit of God dwells in you. But if any man doesn't have the Spirit of Christ, he is not his.

Romans 8:11 But if the Spirit of him who raised up Jesus from the dead dwells in you, he who raised up Christ Jesus from the dead will also give life to your mortal bodies through his Spirit who dwells in you.

Romans 8:13 For if you live after the flesh, you must die; but if by the Spirit you put to death the deeds of the body, you will live.

Romans 8:15 For you didn't receive the spirit of bondage again to fear, but you received the Spirit of adoption, by whom we cry, "Abba! Father!"

Romans 8:26-27 In the same way, the Spirit also helps our weaknesses, for we don't know how to pray as we ought. But the Spirit himself makes intercession for us with groanings which can't be uttered. He who searches the hearts knows what is on the Spirit's mind, because he makes intercession for the saints according to God.

Romans 8:31 What then shall we say about these things? If God is for us, who can be against us?

Romans 12:2 Don't be conformed to this world, but be transformed by the renewing of your mind, so that you may prove what is the good, well-pleasing, and perfect will of God.

Romans 12:10-13 In love of the brothers be tenderly affectionate to one another; in honor preferring one another; not lagging in diligence; fervent in spirit; serving the Lord; rejoicing in hope; enduring in troubles; continuing steadfastly in prayer; contributing to the needs of the saints; given to hospitality.

Romans 13:13-14 Let's walk properly, as in the day; not in reveling and drunkenness, not in sexual promiscuity and lustful acts, and not in strife and jealousy. But put on the Lord Jesus

Christ, and make no provision for the flesh, for its lusts.

Romans 14:8-9 For if we live, we live to the Lord. Or if we die, we die to the Lord. If therefore we live or die, we are the Lord's. For to this end Christ died, rose, and lived again, that he might be Lord of both the dead and the living.

Romans 14:10-11 "But you, why do you judge your brother? Or you again, why do you despise your brother? For we will all stand before the judgment seat of Christ. For it is written, 'As I live,' says the Lord, 'to me every knee will bow. Every tongue will confess to God.'"

Romans 14:20-21 Don't overthrow God's work for food's sake. All things indeed are clean, however it is evil for that man who creates a stumbling block by eating. It is good to not eat meat, drink wine, nor do anything by which your brother stumbles, is offended, or is made weak.

Romans 15:30 Now I beg you, brothers, by our Lord Jesus Christ and by the love of the Spirit, that you strive together with me in your prayers to God for me,

1 Corinthians 2:3-5 I was with you in weakness, in fear, and in much trembling. My speech and my preaching were not in persuasive words of human wisdom, but in demonstration of the Spirit and of power, that your faith wouldn't stand in the wisdom of men, but in the power of God.

1 Corinthians 6:15 Don't you know that your bodies are members of Christ? Shall I then take the members of Christ and make them members of a prostitute? May it never be!

1 Corinthians 6:19-20 Or don't you know that your body is a temple of the Holy Spirit who is in you, whom you have from God? You are not your own, for you were bought with a price. Therefore glorify God in your body and in your spirit, which are God's.

1 Corinthians 11:29-31 For he who eats and drinks in an unworthy way eats and drinks judgment to himself if he doesn't discern the Lord's body. For this cause many among you are weak and sickly, and not a few sleep. For if we discerned ourselves, we wouldn't be judged.

1 Corinthians 12:9 ...to another faith, by the same Spirit; and to another gifts of healings, by the same Spirit;

1 Corinthians 12:28 God has set some in the assembly: first apostles, second prophets, third teachers, then miracle workers, then gifts of healings, helps, governments, and various kinds of languages.

1 Corinthians 13:4-7 Love is patient and is kind. Love doesn't envy. Love doesn't brag, is not proud, doesn't behave itself inappropriately, doesn't seek its own way, is not provoked, takes no account of evil; doesn't rejoice in unrighteousness, but rejoices with the truth; bears all things, believes all things, hopes all things, and endures all things.

1 Corinthians 13:12 For now we see in a mirror, dimly, but then face to face. Now I know in part, but then I will know fully, even as I was also fully known.

1 Corinthians 14:33 ...for God is not a God of confusion, but of peace, as in all the assemblies of the saints.

1 Corinthians 15:20-22 But now Christ has been raised from the dead. He became the first fruit of those who are asleep. For since death came by man, the resurrection of the dead also came by man. For as in Adam all die, so also in Christ all will be made alive.

1 Corinthians 15:42-44 So also is the resurrection of the dead. The body is sown perishable; it is raised imperishable. It is sown in dishonor; it is raised in glory. It is sown in weakness; it is raised in power. It is sown a natural body; it is raised a spiritual body. There is a natural body and there is also a spiritual body.

1 Corinthians 15:57 But thanks be to God, who gives us the victory through our Lord Jesus Christ.

2 Corinthians 1:10 ...who delivered us out of so great a death, and does deliver; on whom we have set our hope that he will also still deliver us;

2 Corinthians 1:20 For however many are the promises of God, in him is the "Yes." Therefore also through him is the "Amen", to the glory of God through us.

2 Corinthians 2:10-11 Now I also forgive whomever you forgive anything. For if indeed I have forgiven anything, I have forgiven that one for your sakes in the presence of Christ, that no advantage may be gained over us by Satan, for we are not ignorant of his schemes.

2 Corinthians 4:3-4 Even if our Good News is veiled, it is veiled in those who are dying, in whom the god of this world has blinded the minds of the unbelieving, that the light of the Good News of the glory of Christ, who is the image of God, should not dawn on them.

2 Corinthians 4:10-11 ...always carrying in the body the putting to death of the Lord Jesus, that the life of Jesus may also be revealed in our body. For we who live are always delivered to death for Jesus' sake, that the life also of Jesus may be revealed in our mortal flesh.

2 Corinthians 4:13 But having the same spirit of faith, according to that which is written, "I believed, and therefore I spoke." We also believe, and therefore we also speak;"

2 Corinthians 4:17-18 For our light affliction, which is for the moment, works for us more and more exceedingly an eternal weight of glory, while we don't look at the things which are seen, but at the things which are not seen. For the things which are seen are temporal, but the things which are not seen are eternal.

2 Corinthians 5:6-7 Therefore we are always confident and know that while we are at home in the body, we are absent from the Lord; for we walk by faith, not by sight.

2 Corinthians 5:21 For him who knew no sin he made to be sin on our behalf; so that in him we might become the righteousness of God.

2 Corinthians 6:2 For he says, "At an acceptable time I listened to you. In a day of salvation I helped you." Behold, now is the acceptable time. Behold, now is the day of salvation.

2 Corinthians 7:4 Great is my boldness of speech toward you. Great is my boasting on your behalf. I am filled with comfort. I overflow with joy in all our affliction.

2 Corinthians 7:5 For even when we had come into Macedonia, our flesh had no relief, but we were afflicted on every side. Fightings were outside. Fear was inside.

2 Corinthians 7:10 For godly sorrow produces repentance to salvation, which brings no regret. But the sorrow of the world produces death.

2 Corinthians 10:3-5 For though we walk in the flesh, we don't wage war according to the flesh; for the weapons of our warfare are not of the flesh, but mighty before God to the throwing down of strongholds, throwing down imaginations and every high thing that is exalted against the knowledge of God and bringing every thought into captivity to the obedience of Christ,

2 Corinthians 12:7-8 By reason of the exceeding greatness of the revelations, that I should not be exalted excessively, a thorn in the flesh was given to me: a messenger of Satan to torment me, that I should not be exalted excessively. Concerning this thing, I begged the Lord three times that it might depart from me.

2 Corinthians 12:9-10 He has said to me, "My grace is sufficient for you, for my power is made perfect in weakness." Most gladly therefore I will rather glory in my weaknesses, that the power of Christ may rest on me. Therefore I take pleasure in weaknesses, in injuries, in necessities, in persecutions, and in distresses, for Christ's sake. For when I am weak, then am I strong.

Galatians 2:20 I have been crucified with Christ, and it is no longer I who live, but Christ lives in me. That life which I now live in the flesh, I live by faith in the Son of God, who loved me, and gave himself up for me.

Galatians 3:1-3 Foolish Galatians, who has bewitched you not to obey the truth, before whose eyes Jesus Christ was openly portrayed among you as crucified? I just want to learn this from you: Did you receive the Spirit by the works of the law, or by hearing of faith? Are you so foolish? Having begun in the Spirit, are you now completed in the flesh?

Galatians 3:13-14 Christ redeemed us from the curse of the law, having become a curse for us. For it is written, "Cursed is everyone who hangs on a tree," that the blessing of Abraham might come on the Gentiles through Christ Jesus, that we might receive the promise of the Spirit through faith.

Galatians 3:29 If you are Christ's, then you are Abraham's offspring and heirs according to promise.

Galatians 5:16 But I say, walk by the Spirit, and you won't fulfill the lust of the flesh.

Galatians 5:19-21 Now the deeds of the flesh are obvious, which are: adultery, sexual immorality, uncleanness, lustfulness, idolatry, sorcery, hatred, strife, jealousies, outbursts of anger, rivalries, divisions, heresies, envy, murders, drunkenness, orgies, and things like these; of which I forewarn you, even as I also forewarned you, that those who practice such things will not inherit God's Kingdom.

Galatians 5:22-23 But the fruit of the Spirit is love, joy, peace, patience, kindness, goodness, faith, gentleness, and self-control. Against such things there is no law.

Galatians 5:24 Those who belong to Christ have crucified the flesh with its passions and lusts.

Galatians 6:5 For each man will bear his own burden.

Galatians 6:7-9 Don't be deceived. God is not mocked, for whatever a man sows, that he will also reap. For he who sows to his own flesh will from the flesh reap corruption. But he who sows to the Spirit will from the Spirit reap eternal life. Let's not be weary in doing good, for we will reap in due season, if we don't give up.

Ephesians 1:5 ...having predestined us for adoption as children through Jesus Christ to himself, according to the good pleasure of his desire,

Ephesians 1:7 ...in whom we have our redemption through his blood, the forgiveness of our trespasses, according to the riches of his grace,

Ephesians 1:21-23 ...far above all rule, authority, power, dominion, and every name that is named, not only in this age, but also in that which is to come. He put all things in subjection under his feet, and gave him to be head over all things for the assembly, which is his body, the fullness of him who fills all in all.

Ephesians 3:20-21 Now to him who is able to do exceedingly abundantly above all that we ask or think, according to the power that works in us, to him be the glory in the assembly and in Christ Jesus to all generations forever and ever. Amen.

Ephesians 4:16 ...from whom all the body, being fitted and knit together through that which every joint supplies, according to the working in measure of each individual part, makes the body increase to the building up of itself in love.

Ephesians 4:17-18 This I say therefore, and testify in the Lord, that you no longer walk as the rest of the Gentiles also walk, in the futility of their mind, being darkened in their understanding, alienated from the life of God because of the ignorance that is in them, because of the hardening of their hearts.

Ephesians 4:22-24 ...that you put away, as concerning your former way of life, the old man that grows corrupt after the lusts of deceit, and that you be renewed in the spirit of your mind, and put on the new man, who in the likeness of God has been created in righteousness and holiness of truth.

Ephesians 4:26-28 "Be angry, and don't sin." Don't let the sun go down on your wrath, and don't give place to the devil. Let him who stole steal no more; but rather let him labor, producing with his hands something that is good, that he may have something to give to him who has need.

Ephesians 4:31-32 Let all bitterness, wrath, anger, outcry, and slander be put away from you, with all malice. And be kind to one another, tender hearted, forgiving each other, just as God also in Christ forgave you.

Ephesians 5:14 Therefore he says, "Awake, you who sleep, and arise from the dead, and Christ will shine on you."

Ephesians 5:18 Don't be drunken with wine, in which is dissipation, but be filled with the Spirit,

Ephesians 5:26 ...that he might sanctify it, having cleansed it by the washing of water with the word,

Ephesians 6:2-3 "Honor your father and mother," which is the first commandment with a promise: "that it may be well with you, and you may live long on the earth."

Ephesians 6:5-6 Servants, be obedient to those who according to the flesh are your masters, with fear and trembling, in singleness of your heart, as to Christ, not in the way of service only when eyes are on you, as men pleasers, but as servants of Christ, doing the will of God from the heart,

Ephesians 6:12 For our wrestling is not against flesh and blood, but against the principalities, against the powers, against the world's rulers of the darkness of this age, and against the spiritual forces of wickedness in the heavenly places.

Ephesians 6:16-17 ...above all, taking up the shield of faith, with which you will be able to quench all the fiery darts of the evil one. And take the helmet of salvation, and the sword of the Spirit, which is the word of God;

Philippians 1:6 ...being confident of this very thing, that he who began a good work in you will complete it until the day of Jesus Christ.

Philippians 1:19 For I know that this will turn out to my salvation, through your prayers and the supply of the Spirit of Jesus Christ,

Philippians 2:1-2 If therefore there is any exhortation in Christ, if any consolation of love, if any fellowship of the Spirit, if any tender mercies and compassion, make my joy full by being like-minded, having the same love, being of one accord, of one mind;

Philippians 2:9-11 Therefore God also highly exalted him, and gave to him the name which is above every name, that at the name of Jesus every knee should bow, of those in heaven, those on earth, and those under the earth, and that every tongue should confess that Jesus Christ is Lord, to the glory of God the Father.

Philippians 2:13 For it is God who works in you both to will and to work, for his good pleasure.

Philippians 2:27 For indeed he was sick, nearly to death, but God had mercy on him, and not on him only, but on me also, that I might not have sorrow on sorrow.

Philippians 3:13 Brothers, I don't regard myself as yet having taken hold, but one thing I do: forgetting the things which are behind, and stretching forward to the things which are before,

Philippians 4:6-8 In nothing be anxious, but in everything, by prayer and petition with thanksgiving, let your requests be made known to God. And the peace of God, which surpasses all understanding, will guard your hearts and your thoughts in Christ Jesus. Finally, brothers, whatever things are true, whatever things are honorable, whatever things are just, whatever things are pure, whatever things are lovely, whatever things are of good report: if there is any virtue and if there is any praise, think about these things.

Philippians 4:13 I can do all things through Christ, who strengthens me.

Colossians 1:10-11 ...that you may walk worthily of the Lord, to please him in all respects, bearing fruit in every good work and increasing in the knowledge of God, strengthened with all power, according to the might of his glory, for all endurance and perseverance with joy,

Colossians 1:13 ...who delivered us out of the power of darkness, and translated us into the Kingdom of the Son of his love,

Colossians 2:2   ...that their hearts may be comforted, they being knit together in love, and gaining all riches of the full assurance of understanding, that they may know the mystery of God, both of the Father and of Christ,

Colossians 2:18-19 Let no one rob you of your prize by self-abasement and worshiping of the angels, dwelling in the things which he has not seen, vainly puffed up by his fleshly mind, and not holding firmly to the Head, from whom all the body, being supplied and knit together through the joints and ligaments, grows with God's growth.

Colossians 3:5-8 Put to death therefore your members which are on the earth: sexual immorality, uncleanness, depraved passion, evil desire, and covetousness, which is idolatry. For these things' sake the wrath of God comes on the children of disobedience. You also once walked in those, when you lived in them; but now you also put them all away: anger, wrath, malice, slander, and shameful speaking out of your mouth.

Colossians 3:12-13 Put on therefore, as God's chosen ones, holy and beloved, a heart of compassion, kindness, lowliness, humility, and perseverance; bearing with one another, and forgiving each other, if any man has a complaint against any; even as Christ forgave you, so you also do.

Colossians 3:14-15 Above all these things, walk in love, which is the bond of perfection. And let the peace of God rule in your hearts, to which also you were called in one body, and be thankful.

Colossians 3:20-21 Children, obey your parents in all things, for this pleases the Lord. Fathers, don't provoke your children, so that they won't be discouraged.

1 Thessalonians 4:3-5 For this is the will of God: your sanctification, that you abstain from sexual immorality, that each one of you know how to control his own body in sanctification and honor, not in the passion of lust, even as the Gentiles who don't know God,

1 Thessalonians 5:5-7 You are all children of light and children of the day. We don't belong to the night, nor to darkness, so then let's not sleep, as the rest do, but let's watch and be sober. For those who sleep, sleep in the night; and those who are drunk are drunk in the night.

1 Thessalonians 5:9-10 For God didn't appoint us to wrath, but to the obtaining of salvation through our Lord Jesus Christ, who died for us, that, whether we wake or sleep, we should live together with him.

2 Thessalonians 1:7 ...and to give relief to you who are afflicted with us, when the Lord Jesus is revealed from heaven with his mighty angels in flaming fire,

2 Thessalonians 1:11-12 To this end we also pray always for you, that our God may count you worthy of your calling, and fulfill every desire of goodness and work of faith with power, that the name of our Lord Jesus may be glorified in you, and you in him, according to the grace of our God and the Lord Jesus Christ.

2 Thessalonians 2:8 Then the lawless one will be revealed, whom the Lord will kill with the breath of his mouth, and destroy by the manifestation of his coming;

1 Timothy 1:8-11 But we know that the law is good, if a person uses it lawfully, as knowing this, that law is not made for a righteous person, but for the lawless and insubordinate, for the ungodly and sinners, for the unholy and profane, for murderers of fathers and murderers of mothers, for manslayers, for the sexually immoral, for homosexuals, for slave-traders, for liars, for perjurers, and for any other thing contrary to the sound doctrine, according to the Good News of the glory of the blessed God, which was committed to my trust.

1 Timothy 1:18-20 I commit this instruction to you, my child Timothy, according to the prophecies which were given to you before, that by them you may wage the good warfare, holding faith and a good conscience, which some having thrust away made a shipwreck concerning the faith, of whom are Hymenaeus and Alexander, whom I delivered to Satan, that they might be taught not to blaspheme.

1 Timothy 4:8 For bodily exercise has some value, but godliness has value in all things, having the promise of the life which is now, and of that which is to come.

1 Timothy 5:23-24 Be no longer a drinker of water only, but use a little wine for your stomach's sake and your frequent infirmities. Some men's sins are evident, preceding them to judgment, and some also follow later.

1 Timothy 6:6 But godliness with contentment is great gain.

1 Timothy 6:10 For the love of money is a root of all kinds of evil. Some have been led astray from the faith in their greed, and have pierced themselves through with many sorrows.

1 Timothy 6:11-12 But you, man of God, flee these things, and follow after righteousness, godliness, faith, love, perseverance, and gentleness. Fight the good fight of faith. Take hold of the eternal life to which you were called, and you confessed the good confession in the sight of many witnesses.

2 Timothy 1:7 For God didn't give us a spirit of fear, but of power, love, and self-control.

2 Timothy 2:22 Flee from youthful lusts; but pursue righteousness, faith, love, and peace with those who call on the Lord out of a pure heart.

2 Timothy 2:24-26 The Lord's servant must not quarrel, but be gentle toward all, able to teach, patient, in gentleness correcting those who oppose him: perhaps God may give them repentance leading to a full knowledge of the truth, and they may recover themselves out of the devil's snare, having been taken captive by him to his will.

2 Timothy 3:4-5 ...traitors, headstrong, conceited, lovers of pleasure rather than lovers of God, holding a form of godliness, but having denied its power. Turn away from these, also.

2 Timothy 3:7 ...always learning, and never able to come to the knowledge of the truth.

2 Timothy 4:18 And the Lord will deliver me from every evil work, and will preserve me for his heavenly Kingdom. To him be the glory forever and ever. Amen.

Titus 2:6-8 Likewise, exhort the younger men to be sober minded. In all things show yourself an example of good works. In your teaching, show integrity, seriousness, incorruptibility, and soundness of speech that can't be condemned, that he who opposes you may be ashamed, having no evil thing to say about us.

Titus 2:11-14 For the grace of God has appeared, bringing salvation to all men, instructing us to the intent that, denying ungodliness and worldly lusts, we would live soberly, righteously, and godly in this present age; looking for the blessed hope and appearing of the glory of our great God and Savior, Jesus Christ, who gave himself for us, that he might redeem us from all iniquity, and purify for himself a people for his own possession, zealous for good works.

Titus 3:10-11 Avoid a factious man after a first and second warning, knowing that such a one is perverted and sins, being self-condemned.

Hebrews 2:9 But we see him who has been made a little lower than the angels, Jesus, because of the suffering of death crowned with glory and honor, that by the grace of God he should taste of death for everyone.

Hebrews 2:14 Since then the children have shared in flesh and blood, he also himself in the same way partook of the same, that through death he might bring to nothing him who had the power of death, that is, the devil,

Hebrews 2:15 ...and might deliver all of them who through fear of death were all their lifetime subject to bondage.

Hebrews 4:9-11 There remains therefore a Sabbath rest for the people of God. For he who has entered into his rest has himself also rested from his works, as God did from his. Let's therefore give diligence to enter into that rest, lest anyone fall after the same example of disobedience.

Hebrews 4:12-13 For the word of God is living and active, and sharper than any two-edged sword, piercing even to the dividing of soul and spirit, of both joints and marrow, and is able to discern the thoughts and intentions of the heart. There is no creature that is hidden from his sight, but all things are naked and laid open before the eyes of him to whom we must give an account.

Hebrews 4:15 For we don't have a high priest who can't be touched with the feeling of our infirmities, but one who has been in all points tempted like we are, yet without sin.

Hebrews 5:7-8 He, in the days of his flesh, having offered up prayers and petitions with strong crying and tears to him who was able to save him from death, and having been heard for his godly fear, though he was a Son, yet learned obedience by the things which he suffered.

Hebrews 5:14 But solid food is for those who are full grown, who by reason of use have their senses exercised to discern good and evil.

Hebrews 6:11-14 We desire that each one of you may show the same diligence to the fullness of hope even to the end, that you won't be sluggish, but imitators of those who through faith and perseverance inherited the promises. For when God made a promise to Abraham, since he could swear by no one greater, he swore by himself, saying, "Surely blessing I will bless you, and multiplying I will multiply you."

Hebrews 6:17-18 In this way God, being determined to show more abundantly to the heirs of the promise the immutability of his counsel, interposed with an oath, that by two immutable things, in which it is impossible for God to lie, we may have a strong encouragement, who have fled for refuge to take hold of the hope set before us.

Hebrews 8:6 But now he has obtained a more excellent ministry, by so much as he is also the mediator of a better covenant, which on better promises has been given as law.

Hebrews 9:27-28 Inasmuch as it is appointed for men to die once, and after this, judgment, so Christ also, having been offered once to bear the sins of many, will appear a second time, without sin, to those who are eagerly waiting for him for salvation.

Hebrews 10:22-23 ...let's draw near with a true heart in fullness of faith, having our hearts sprinkled from an evil conscience, and having our body washed with pure water, let's hold fast the confession of our hope without wavering; for he who promised is faithful.

Hebrews 10:26-27 For if we sin willfully after we have received the knowledge of the truth, there remains no more a sacrifice for sins, but a certain fearful expectation of judgment, and a fierceness of fire which will devour the adversaries.

Hebrews 10:35 Therefore don't throw away your boldness, which has a great reward.

Hebrews 11:6 Without faith it is impossible to be well pleasing to him, for he who comes to God must believe that he exists, and that he is a rewarder of those who seek him.

Hebrews 11:11 By faith, even Sarah herself received power to conceive, and she bore a child when she was past age, since she counted him faithful who had promised.

Hebrews 11:32-34 What more shall I say? For the time would fail me if I told of Gideon, Barak, Samson, Jephthah, David, Samuel, and the prophets, who through faith subdued kingdoms, worked out righteousness, obtained promises, stopped the mouths of lions, quenched the power of fire, escaped the edge of the sword, from weakness were made strong, grew mighty in war, and caused foreign armies to flee.

Hebrews 12:2 Therefore lift up the hands that hang down and the feeble knees,

Hebrews 12:11-13 All chastening seems for the present to be not joyous but grievous; yet afterward it yields the peaceful fruit of righteousness to those who have been trained by it. Therefore lift up the hands that hang down and the feeble knees, and make straight paths for your feet, so what is lame may not be dislocated, but rather be healed.

Hebrews 12:14-16 Follow after peace with all men, and the sanctification without which no man will see the Lord, looking carefully lest there be any man who falls short of the grace of God, lest any root of bitterness springing up trouble you, and many be defiled by it, lest there be any sexually immoral person, or profane person, like Esau, who sold his birthright for one meal.

Hebrews 12:28-29 Therefore, receiving a Kingdom that can't be shaken, let's have grace, through which we serve God acceptably, with reverence and awe, for our God is a consuming fire.

Hebrews 13:6 So that with good courage we say, "The Lord is my helper. I will not fear. What can man do to me?"

Hebrews 13:8 Jesus Christ is the same yesterday, today, and forever.

James 1:5 But if any of you lacks wisdom, let him ask of God, who gives to all liberally and without reproach, and it will be given to him.

James 1:26-27 If anyone among you thinks himself to be religious while he doesn't bridle his tongue, but deceives his heart, this man's religion is worthless. Pure religion and undefiled before our God and Father is this: to visit the fatherless and widows in their affliction, and to keep oneself unstained by the world.

James 2:5 Listen, my beloved brothers. Didn't God choose those who are poor in this world to be rich in faith, and heirs of the Kingdom which he promised to those who love him?

James 3:6 And the tongue is a fire. The world of iniquity among our members is the tongue, which defiles the whole body, and sets on fire the course of nature, and is set on fire by Gehenna.

James 3:8 ...but nobody can tame the tongue. It is a restless evil, full of deadly poison.

James 3:16 For where jealousy and selfish ambition are, there is confusion and every evil deed.

James 3:17 But the wisdom that is from above is first pure, then peaceful, gentle, reasonable, full of mercy and good fruits, without partiality, and without hypocrisy.

James 4:2-4 You lust, and don't have. You murder and covet, and can't obtain. You fight and make war. You don't have, because you don't ask. You ask, and don't receive, because you ask with wrong motives, so that you may spend it on your pleasures. You adulterers and adulteresses, don't you know that friendship with the world is hostility toward God? Whoever therefore wants to be a friend of the world makes himself an enemy of God.

James 4:7-8 Be subject therefore to God. Resist the devil, and he will flee from you. Draw near to God, and he will draw near to you. Cleanse your hands, you sinners. Purify your hearts, you double-minded.

James 5:9 Don't grumble, brothers, against one another, so that you won't be judged. Behold, the judge stands at the door.

James 5:14 Is any among you sick? Let him call for the elders of the assembly, and let them pray over him, anointing him with oil in the name of the Lord,

James 5:15 ...and the prayer of faith will heal him who is sick, and the Lord will raise him up. If he has committed sins, he will be forgiven.

James 5:16 Confess your offenses to one another, and pray for one another, that you may be healed. The insistent prayer of a righteous person is powerfully effective.

1 Peter 1:3-4 Blessed be the God and Father of our Lord Jesus Christ, who according to his great mercy caused us to be born again to a living hope through the resurrection of Jesus Christ from the dead, to an incorruptible and undefiled inheritance that doesn't fade away, reserved in Heaven for you,

1 Peter 2:24 He himself bore our sins in his body on the tree, that we, having died to sins, might live to righteousness. You were healed by his wounds.

1 Peter 3:3-4 Let your beauty be not just the outward adorning of braiding the hair, and of wearing jewels of gold, or of putting on fine clothing; but in the hidden person of the heart, in the incorruptible adornment of a gentle and quiet spirit, which is very precious in the sight of God.

1 Peter 3:8-9 Finally, all of you be like-minded, compassionate, loving as brothers, tenderhearted, courteous, not rendering evil for evil, or insult for insult; but instead blessing, knowing that you were called to this, that you may inherit a blessing.

1 Peter 3:10-11 For, "He who would love life and see good days, let him keep his tongue from evil and his lips from speaking deceit. Let him turn away from evil and do good. Let him seek peace and pursue it."

1 Peter 4:13-14 But because you are partakers of Christ's sufferings, rejoice, that at the revelation of his glory you also may rejoice with exceeding joy. If you are insulted for the name of Christ, you are blessed; because the Spirit of glory and of God rests on you. On their part he is blasphemed, but on your part he is glorified.

1 Peter 5:7-9 ...casting all your worries on him, because he cares for you. Be sober and self-controlled. Be watchful. Your adversary, the devil, walks around like a roaring lion, seeking whom he may devour. Withstand him steadfast in your faith, knowing that your brothers who are in the world are undergoing the same sufferings.

2 Peter 1:3   ...seeing that his divine power has granted to us all things that pertain to life and godliness, through the knowledge of him who called us by his own glory and virtue,

1 John 1:9 If we confess our sins, he is faithful and righteous to forgive us the sins, and to cleanse us from all unrighteousness.

1 John 2:15-16 Don't love the world or the things that are in the world. If anyone loves the world, the Father's love isn't in him. For all that is in the world, the lust of the flesh, the lust of the eyes, and the pride of life, isn't the Father's, but is the world's.

1 John 3:17 But whoever has the world's goods and sees his brother in need, then closes his heart of compassion against him, how does God's love remain in him?

1 John 3:21-22   Beloved, if our hearts don't condemn us, we have boldness toward God; so whatever we ask, we receive from him, because we keep his commandments and do the things that are pleasing in his sight.

1 John 4:1   Beloved, don't believe every spirit, but test the spirits, whether they are of God, because many false prophets have gone out into the world.

1 John 4:18   There is no fear in love; but perfect love casts out fear, because fear has punishment. He who fears is not made perfect in love.

1 John 4:20-21   If a man says, "I love God," and hates his brother, he is a liar; for he who doesn't love his brother whom he has seen, how can he love God whom he has not seen? This commandment we have from him, that he who loves God should also love his brother.

1 John 5:3   For this is loving God, that we keep his commandments. His commandments are not grievous.

1 John 5:4 For whatever is born of God overcomes the world. This is the victory that has overcome the world: your faith.

1 John 5:14-15 This is the boldness which we have toward him, that if we ask anything according to his will, he listens to us. And if we know that he listens to us, whatever we ask, we know that we have the petitions which we have asked of him.

3 John 2 Beloved, I pray that you may prosper in all things and be healthy, even as your soul prospers.

Jude 1:5 Now I desire to remind you, though you already know this, that the Lord, having saved a people out of the land of Egypt, afterward destroyed those who didn't believe.

Jude 1:24-25 Now to him who is able to keep them from stumbling, and to present you faultless before the presence of his glory in great joy, to God our Savior, who alone is wise, be glory and majesty, dominion and power, both now and forever. Amen.

Revelation 2:7 "He who has an ear, let him hear what the Spirit says to the assemblies. To him who overcomes I will give to eat from the tree of life, which is in the Paradise of my God."

Revelation 3:10 "Because you kept my command to endure, I also will keep you from the hour of testing which is to come on the whole world, to test those who dwell on the earth."

Revelation 3:18 "I counsel you to buy from me gold refined by fire, that you may become rich; and white garments, that you may clothe yourself, and that the shame of your nakedness may not be revealed; and eye salve to anoint your eyes, that you may see."

Revelation 3:19-20 "As many as I love, I reprove and chasten. Be zealous therefore, and repent. Behold, I stand at the door and knock. If anyone hears my voice and opens the door, then I will come in to him, and will dine with him, and he with me."

Revelation 12:11 They overcame him because of the Lamb's blood, and because of the word of their testimony. They didn't love their life, even to death.

Revelation 14:11 The smoke of their torment goes up forever and ever. They have no rest day and night, those who worship the beast and his image, and whoever receives the mark of his name.

Revelation 18:4-5 I heard another voice from heaven, saying, "Come out of her, my people, that you have no participation in her sins, and that you don't receive of her plagues, for her sins have reached to the sky, and God has remembered her iniquities."

Revelation 21:4 "He will wipe away every tear from their eyes. Death will be no more; neither will there be mourning, nor crying, nor pain, any more. The first things have passed away."

Revelation 21:6 He said to me, "I am the Alpha and the Omega, the Beginning and the End. I will give freely to him who is thirsty from the spring of the water of life."

Revelation 21:7-8 "He who overcomes, I will give him these things. I will be his God, and he will be my son. But for the cowardly, unbelieving, sinners, abominable, murderers, sexually immoral, sorcerers, idolaters, and all liars, their part is in the lake that burns with fire and sulfur, which is the second death."

Revelation 22:1-2 He showed me a river of water of life, clear as crystal, proceeding out of the throne of God and of the Lamb, in the middle of its street. On this side of the river and on that was the tree of life, bearing twelve kinds of fruits, yielding its fruit every month. The leaves of the tree were for the healing of the nations.

Revelation 22:14-16 "Blessed are those who do his commandments, that they may have the right to the tree of life, and may enter in by the gates into the city. Outside are the dogs, the sorcerers, the sexually immoral, the murderers, the idolaters, and everyone who loves and practices falsehood. I, Jesus, have sent my angel to testify these things to you for the assemblies. I am the root and the offspring of David, the Bright and Morning Star."

Revelation 22:17 The Spirit and the bride say, "Come!" He who hears, let him say, "Come!" He who is thirsty, let him come. He who desires, let him take the water of life freely.

General Index

Affliction

Exodus 4:31, 2 Chronicles 18:26, Job 34:28, Job 36:8-10, Psalm 25:18, Psalm 34:19, Psalm 39:10-11, Psalm 119:50, Psalm 119:65-67, Psalm 119:153, Proverbs 15:15, Isaiah 58:10, Jeremiah 9:7, Jeremiah 16:19, Lamentations 1:3, Lamentations 1:9, Ezekiel 6:9-10, Micah 4:6-7, Nahum 1:7-9, Mark 5:29, 2 Corinthians 1:4, 2 Corinthians 7:4, 2 Corinthians 7:5, 2 Corinthians 4:17-18, Galatians 6:5, 2 Thessalonians 1:7, James 1:26-27

Addiction (includes Drink, Drunk, Sober)

Psalm 107:27-28, Proverbs 20:1, Proverbs 21:21, Proverbs 26:8-9, Romans 13:13-14, Galatians 5:19-21, Ephesians 5:18, 1 Thessalonians 5:5-7

Anxiety and Stress

Exodus 14:14, Joshua 1:9, Psalm 27:1-2, Psalm 37:7-9, Psalm 61:2, Psalm 69:29, Psalm 94:19, Psalm 107:27-28, Psalm 121:1-2, Proverbs 3:5-6, Proverbs 12:25, Proverbs 29:22-25, Isaiah 41:10, Isaiah 43:1-3, Matthew 6:25, Matthew 6:34, Matthew 8:26, Matthew 11:28-30, Mark 5:36, Luke 10:41-42, John 14:1, John 14:27, John 16:33, Romans 8:31, Philippians 4:6-8, Colossians 3:12-15, Hebrews 13:6, 1 Peter 5:7-9

Authority

Numbers 5:20-22, Matthew 8:9-10, Matthew 9:6-7, Matthew 10:1, Luke 4:35-36, Luke 9:1-2, Luke 10:19, Ephesians 1:21-23

Barrenness

Genesis 18:14, Genesis 20:17, Genesis 25:21, Exodus 23:26, 1 Samuel 1:4-5, 2 Kings 2:21-22, Psalm 113:9, Psalm 127:3, Isaiah 54:1, Luke 1:36, Hebrews 11:11

Believe/Belief (includes Unbelief)

Exodus 4:31, Psalm 106: 24-25, Psalm 119:65-67, Matthew 7:10-12, Matthew 8:13, Matthew 9:28-30,

Matthew 18:6, Mark 5:36, Mark 9:23-24, Mark 11:22-24, Mark 16:17-18, Mark 16:14, Luke 8:50, John 3:16, John 5:24, John 6:33-35, John 11:25, John 11:42-44, John 14:1, John 14:12-14, Romans 4:17, 1 Corinthians 13:4-7, 2 Corinthians 4:13, 2 Timothy 3:4-5, Hebrews 11:6, Hebrews 12:28-29, Jude 1:5, Revelation 21:7-8

Blind/Blindness (see Eyes)

Blood

Exodus 12:13, Psalm 72:14, Hosea 4:2-3, Matthew 26:27-28, Mark 5:29, 1 Corinthians 11:29-31, Ephesians 1:7, Ephesians 6:12, Hebrews 2:14, Revelation 12:11

Body

Romans 6:13, 1 Corinthians 6:15, 1 Corinthians 6:19-20, Ephesians 4:16, Colossians 2:2, Colossians 2:18-19, Colossians 3:12-13, 1 Thessalonians 4:3-5, Hebrews 4:12-13

Boils (see Skin)

Bones (includes Marrow, Joints)

Genesis 32:25, Job 10:11-12, Job 19:20, Job 30:30, Psalm 6:2, Psalm 22:14, Psalm 31:10, Psalm 32:3-5, Psalm 34:20, Psalm 35:9-10, Psalm 38:3, Psalm 51:8, Psalm 63:5, Psalm 102:3-5, Psalm 109:22-24, Proverbs 3:7-8, Proverbs 7:23, Proverbs 12:4, Proverbs 14:30, Proverbs 15:30, Proverbs 17:22, Proverbs 25:15, Proverbs 25:19, Isaiah 38:13-14, Lamentations 1:13, Ezekiel 37:11-12, Luke 13:12-13, Ephesians 4:16, Colossians 2:19, Hebrews 4:12-13

Breath (includes Breathe)

Job 33:4, Psalm 39:4-5, Psalm 39:10-11, Ezekiel 37:5, Ezekiel 37:6, Ezekiel 37:9, Acts 17:25, 2 Thessalonians 2:8

Bruise

Proverbs 23:29-30, Isaiah 53:10

Bowels (includes Stomach)

Numbers 5:20-22, 2 Chronicles 21:15, Psalm 38:7, Psalm 109:17-18, Proverbs 7:25, Proverbs 18:8, Proverbs 18:20, Proverbs 25:15, Isaiah 38:13-14, Ezekiel 3:3, John 6:33-35, 1 Corinthians 11:29-31

Compassion

Matthew 14:14, Mark 1:40-42, Luke 10:33-34, 1 John 3:17

Confusion (see also Mind)

Deuteronomy 21:5, Deuteronomy 28:20, Daniel 9:8, Acts 3:16, 1 Corinthians 14:33, James 3:16

Covenant

Numbers 17:10, Psalm 89:34, Hebrews 8:6

Cure

Jeremiah 33:6, Matthew 17:15-18, Luke 7:21, Luke 9:1-2, Luke 9:11, Acts 28:8-9

Curse

Leviticus 19:30-31, Numbers 5:20-22, Deuteronomy 23:5, Deuteronomy 30:19-20, Jeremiah 17:5, Psalm 7:14-16, Psalm 109:17-18, Proverbs 26:2, Acts 13:10-11, Galatians 3:13-14

Deafness (see Ears)

Death (Includes Resurrection)

Numbers 17:10, 2 Kings 4:19, 32, 33; 2 Kings 4:35, Psalm 23:4, Psalm 39:4-5, Psalm 55:4-5, Psalm 56:13, Psalm 107:20, Psalm 116:3-4, Psalm 116:8-9, Proverbs 14:12, Proverbs 18:21, Ecclesiastes 3:1-2, Hosea 13:14, Matthew 16:28, Luke 8:52-54, John 5:24, Acts 9:40, Acts 12:23, Romans 4:17, Romans 6:4, Romans 7:24-25, Romans 8:2, Romans 8:6, Romans 8:11, Romans 14:8-9, 1 Corinthians 15:20-22, 1 Corinthians 15:42-44, 2 Corinthians 1:10, 2 Corinthians 4:10-11, Hebrews 2:9, Hebrews 2:14, Hebrews 2:15

Deliverance (includes Delivered)

Psalm 25:2, Psalm 25:7, Psalm 25:2022, Psalm 33:18-19, Psalm 34:4, Psalm 34:15-16, Psalm 39:10-11, Psalm 40:2-3, Psalm 66:16-19, Psalm 72:14, Psalm 89:20-23, Psalm 103:19, Psalm 106:4-5, Psalm 107:27-28, Psalm 116:3-4, Psalm 116:8-9, Psalm 118:6-7, Psalm 119:153, Psalm 119:170-173, Psalm 146:7, Psalm 149:6-9, Isaiah 38:16-17, Matthew 9:32-33, John 11:10, 2 Corinthians 1:10, 2 Corinthians 4:10-11

Demons (includes Demonic spirits)

1 Chronicles 10:13-14, Job 2:7, Psalm 34:18, Proverbs 16:18, Proverbs 29:22-25, Proverbs 30:14, Proverbs 30:17, Isaiah 8:19-20, Matthew 4:24, Matthew 6:13, Matthew 8:15-16, Matthew 9:32-33, Matthew 10:1, Matthew 12:22, Matthew 15:22-29, Matthew 17:15, 18; Matthew 18:34, Mark 1:34, Mark 6:13, Mark 9:17, Mark 9:25, Mark 16:17-18, Luke 4:35-36, Luke 4:39, Luke 6:18, Luke 7:21, Luke 8:2, Luke 8:29, Luke 8:36, Luke 9:1-2, Luke 10:19, Luke 11:14, Luke 11:20-23, Luke 11:24-26, Luke 13:12-13, Acts 5:16, Acts 19:12, Romans 8:15, 2 Corinthians 2:10-11, 2 Corinthians 4:3-4, 2 Corinthians 10:3-5, 2 Corinthians 12:7-8, Galatians 3:1-3, Ephesians 6:12, Ephesians 6:16-17, Colossians 3:5-8, 1 Timothy 1:18-20, 2 Timothy 1:7, 2 timothy 3:4-5, 2 Timothy 4:18, Hebrews 2:15, 1 John 4:1

Depression (includes Despair)

Psalm 18:28-30, Psalm 40:2-3, Psalm 43:5, Psalm 55:22, Psalm 69:29, Psalm 71:20-21, Palm 143:3-4, Psalm 143:7-8, Isaiah 54:14, Isaiah 61:1-3, Luke 4:18-19

Disease (see also Plagues)

Exodus 15:26, Deuteronomy 7:15, Deuteronomy 28:58-60, 2 Chronicles 16:12, 2 Chronicles 21:15, Psalm 103:3, Ecclesiastes 6:1-2, Matthew 4:23, Matthew 4:24, Matthew 8:17, Matthew 9:35, Mark 1:34, Mark 3:10, Luke 4:40, Luke 6:17, Luke 7:21, John 5:4, Acts 19:12, Acts 28:8-9

Ears (includes Deaf, Hear)

Job 33:14-16, Job 36:8-10, Psalm 81:11-12, Psalm 106:24-25, Proverbs 15:31, Isaiah 6:9-10, Isaiah 32:4, Isaiah 35:4-5, Matthew 13:15, Matthew 13:16, Mark 7:33-35, Mark 7:37, Mark 9:25, Luke 5:15, Luke 7:22, Revelation 2:7

Epileptic

Matthew 4:24, Matthew 17:15, 18

Eyes (includes Blind, Sight)

Deuteronomy 34:7, 2 Kings 6:17, Job 17:7, Psalm 11:4, Psalm 17:15, Psalm 18:28-30, Psalm 25:15, Psalm 101:3, Psalm 116:8-9, Psalm 119:18, Psalm 119:37, Psalm 121:1-2, Psalm 145:15-16, Psalm 146:8, Proverbs 4:24-25, Proverbs 10:10, Proverbs 12:18, Proverbs 15:3, Proverbs 15:30, Proverbs 16:2, Proverbs 23:6-7, Proverbs 23:26, Proverbs 23:29-30, Proverbs 30:17, Isaiah 5:21, Isaiah 6:9-10,

Isaiah 32:4, Isaiah 35:4-5, Isaiah 38:13-14, Isaiah 42:16, Joel 2:28, Matthew 6:22-23, Matthew 7:1-4, Matthew 9:28-30, Matthew 12:22, Matthew 13:15, Matthew 13:16, Matthew 15:29-31, Matthew 20:30, 32-34, Matthew 21:14, Matthew 26:41, Mark 8:25, Mark 10:52, Luke 4:18-19, Luke 7:22, Luke 18:42, John 9:1-3, John 9:31-32, Acts 9:12, Acts 9:18, Acts 13:10-11, Acts 26:18, 1 Corinthians 13:12, 2 Corinthians 4:3-4, 2 Corinthians 4:17-18, 2 Corinthians 5:6-7, Revelation 3:18

Fear (see also Demons)

Deuteronomy 3:22, Deuteronomy 31:6, 1 Samuel 43:1, Job 11:14-16, Psalm 27:1-2, Psalm 27:3, Psalm 34:4, Psalm 34:7, Psalm 55:4-5, Psalm 56:3, Psalm 91:5-6, Psalm 103:13-14, Psalm 112:7-8, Psalm 118:6-7, Proverbs 29:22-25, Isaiah 35:4-5, Isaiah 43:1-3, Isaiah 54:4, Isaiah 54:14, Jeremiah 29:11, Matthew 8:26, Matthew 10:30-31, Mark 5:36, John 14:27, Romans 8:15, 2 Corinthians 7:5, Philippians 4:13, 2 Timothy 1:7, Hebrews 2:15, Hebrews 5:7-8, Hebrews 10:26-27, Hebrews 13:6, 1 John 4:18

Feet (includes Lame, Walk, Fall, Stumble)

1 Samuel 2:9-10, 2 Samuel 22:37, 2 Chronicles 16:12, Job 2:7, Psalm 17:5, Psalm 18:32-34, Psalm 25:15, Psalm 37:24, Psalm 56:13, Psalm 73:2,

Psalm 91:11-12, Psalm 116:8-9, Psalm 119:32, Proverbs 3:21-23, Proverbs 6:20-22, Proverbs 6:28-29, Proverbs 9:6, Proverbs 10:10, Proverbs 16:18, Proverbs 24:16-18, Proverbs 25:19, Proverbs 26:6-7, Isaiah 1:4-6, Isaiah 35:6, Isaiah 41:13, Lamentations 1:13, Micah 4:6-7, Matthew 15:29-31, Matthew 21:14, Luke 7:22, Luke 14:2-4, Acts 3:11, Acts 14:8-10, Romans 13:13-14, Colossians 1:10-11, Colossians 3:5-8, Colossians 3:12-13, 1 Timothy 6:11-12, Hebrews 12:11-13, Jude 1:24-25

Fever (see also Demons)

Deuteronomy 28:22, Matthew 8:15-16, Mark 1:31, Luke 4:39

Flesh (see also Skin)

Psalm 27:1-2, Psalm 145:21, Jeremiah 17:5, Romans 7:24-25, Romans 8:6, Romans 8:9, Romans 13:13-14, 2 Corinthians 7:5, 2 Corinthians 10:3-5, 2 Corinthians 12:7-8, Galatians 5:16, Galatians 5:19-21, Galatians 5:24, Galatians 6:5-6, Galatians 6:7-9, Ephesians 6:5-6, Ephesians 6:12, Colossians 2:18-19, Colossians 3:5-8, Colossians 3:12-13, 1 Thessalonians 4:3-5, 2 Timothy 2:22, 1 John 2:15-16

Food & Drink (see also Hunger & Thirst)

Exodus 23:25, Psalm 102:3-5, Psalm 145:15-16, Psalm 146:7, Proverbs 17:1, Proverbs 23:6-7, Proverbs 23:21, Proverbs 24:13-14, Proverbs 26:6-7, Matthew 4:4, Mark 7:15, John 6:57, Acts 2:46, Romans 14:20-21, 1 Timothy 5:23-24, Hebrews 5:14, Hebrews 12:12-13, Revelation 2:7, Revelation 3:19-20

Forgive/Forgiveness

1 Kings 8:37-39, 2 Chronicles 7:14, Psalm 19:12, Psalm 25:7, Psalm 25:18, Psalm 32:1-2, Psalm 103:3, Psalm 103:12, Matthew 6:14-15, Matthew 9:2, Matthew 9:6-7, Mark 2:3-5, Acts 2:38, 2 Corinthians 2:10-11, Ephesians 1:7, Ephesians 4:31-32, James 4:7-8, James 5:15, 1 John 1:9, Revelation 3:19-20

Fracture

Deuteronomy 6:4, Isaiah 30:26

Grief (see Mourning, Sorrow)

Hand/Hands

1 Samuel 23:16, 1 Chronicles 29:11-12, Psalm 18:32-34, Psalm 26:6-7, Psalm 63:3-4, Psalm 89:20-23, Proverbs 12:13-14, Isaiah 13:7-8, Isaiah 35:3, Isaiah 41:13, Ezekiel 7:15-18, Mark 3:5, Mark 6:4-5, Acts 4:30, Acts 9:12, Acts 17:25, Acts 28:8-9, Hebrews 12:11-13, James 4:7-8

Head (see also Mind)

2 Kings 4:19, 32, 33; 1 Chronicles 29:11-12, Psalm 7:14-16, Psalm 23:5, Psalm 38:4-5, Proverbs 9:6, Isaiah 1:4-6, Ezekiel 7:15-18, Matthew 10:30-31, Ephesians 1:21-23

Healing (includes Heal, Heals)

Proverbs 13:17, Ecclesiastes 3:3, Isaiah 19:22, Isaiah 58:8, Ezekiel 47:12, Malachi 4:2, Matthew 4:23, Matthew 8:7, Matthew 9:35, Matthew 10:8, Matthew 12:10-13, Matthew 13:15, Matthew 14:14, Matthew 20:30-34, Mark 3:5, Mark 5:29, Mark 6:4-5, Mark 7:33-35, Luke 4:39, Luke 8:2, Luke 8:36, Luke 8:47, Luke 8:50, Luke 9:1-2, Luke 9:6, Luke 9:11, John 5:8-9, John 5:14, Acts 4:22, Acts 10:38, Acts 14:8-10, 1 Corinthians 12:9, 1 Corinthians 12:28, Hebrews 12:12-13, Revelation 22:1-2

Hear (see Ears)

Heart

Leviticus 19:17, 1 Kings 8:37-39, Psalm 4:4, Psalm 5:9, Psalm 12:2-4, Psalm 16:9, Psalm 17:9-10, Psalm 19:14, Psalm 22:14, Psalm 27:3, Psalm 31:23-24, Psalm 34:18, Psalm 51:10, Psalm 55:4-5, Psalm 61:2, Psalm 69:29, Psalm 73:21, Psalm 73:26, Psalm 81:11-12, Psalm 95:8-9, Psalm 102:3-5, Psalm 104:14-15, Psalm 109:22-24, Psalm 112:7-8, Psalm 119:32, Psalm 139:23, Palm 143:3-4, Psalm 147:3, Proverbs 3:5-6, Proverbs 10:18-20, Proverbs 13:12, Proverbs 15:13, Proverbs 15:15, Proverbs 15:30, Proverbs 16:2, Proverbs 16:24, Proverbs 17:22, Proverbs 22:11, Proverbs 23:6-7, Proverbs 23:26, Proverbs 24:16-18, Isaiah 13:7-8, Isaiah 44:20, Isaiah 61:1-3, Jeremiah 17:5, Jeremiah 17:9-10, Ezekiel 6:9-10, Ezekiel 36:26, Matthew 11:28-30, Matthew 13:15, Matthew 22:37-40, Mark 3:5, Mark 12:29-31, Mark 16:14, Luke 4:18-19, John 14:1, John 14:27, Acts 2:26, Acts 2:46, Romans 1:24-25, Ephesians 4:17-18, Ephesians 4:32, Ephesians 6:5-6, Colossians 2:2, Colossians 3:12-13, James 1:27-27, James 4:7-8, 1 Peter 5:3-4, 1 John 3:17, 1 John 3:21-22

Heaviness

Psalm 69:29, Proverbs 15:4, Matthew 11:28-30, Galatians 6:5

Hope

Psalm 43:5, Proverbs 13:12, Proverbs 24:13-14, Jeremiah 29:11, Lamentations 3:22-24, Ezekiel 37:11-12, Matthew 7:7-9, Acts 2:26, Romans 5:3-4, 1 Corinthians 13:4-7, 2 Corinthians 1:10, Titus 2:11-14, Hebrews6:11-14, Hebrews 6:17-18, Hebrews 10:22-23, 1 Peter 1:3-4

Hunger/Thirst (see also Food)

Exodus 23:25, Psalm 104:14-15, Psalm 127:2, Proverbs 19:15, Ezekiel 7:15-18, Ezekiel 47:12, Matthew 4:4, Luke 6:21, John 6:33-35, John 6:57-58, Romans 14:20-21, Revelation 21:6, Revelation 22:17

Infirmity

Matthew 8:17, Matthew 9:12, Luke 5:15, Luke 8:2, Luke 13:11-13, 1 Timothy 5:23-24

Injured (see also Wound)

Proverbs 7:23, Isaiah 1:4-6, Jeremiah 30:17, Matthew 15:29-31

Iniquity (includes Sin)

Genesis 4:7, Nehemiah 9:2, Job 11:14-16, Job 36:8-10, Job 41:34, Psalm 7:14-16, Psalm 31:10, Psalm 32:1-2, Psalm 32:3-5, Psalm 38:17-18, Psalm 39:10-11, Psalm 51:5-6, Psalm 78:36-42, Psalm 89:31-32, Proverbs 6:28-29, Isaiah 1:4-6, Isaiah 53:6, Jeremiah 3:22, Jeremiah 30:15, Ezekiel 7:15-18, Hosea 13:12-13, Matthew 26:27-28, Mark 7:15, John 5:14, John 9:1-3, Acts 26:18, Romans 1:24-25, Romans 1:26-27, Romans 2:1, Romans 5:21, Romans 6:13, Romans 7:22-23, Romans 7:24-25, Romans 14:10-11, Galatians 3:1-3, Ephesians 4:31-32, 1 Thessalonians 4:3-5, 1 Timothy 1:8-11, 1 Timothy 5:23-24, 1 Timothy 6:10, 2 Timothy 2:22, 2 Timothy 2:24-26, 2 Timothy 3:7, Titus 2:11-14, Titus 3:10-11, Hebrews 4:12-13, Hebrews 4:15, Hebrews 9:27-28, Hebrews 10:26-27, Hebrews 12:12-13, James 3:6, 1 John 2:15-16, 1 John 4:20-21, Revelation 21:7-8

Itch

Leviticus 14:53-55

Joints (see Bones)

Joy

Nehemiah 8:10, Psalm 5:11, Psalm 16:11, Psalm 32:10-11, Psalm 35:9-10, Psalm 45:7, Psalm 51:8, Psalm 106:4-5, Isaiah 12:2-3, Jeremiah 31:13, John 15:11, 2 Corinthians 7:4, Galatians 5:22-23, Philippians 2:1-2, Colossians 1:10-11, 1 Peter 4:13-14, Jude 1:24-25

Knees

Psalm 109:22-24, Isaiah 35:3, Ezekiel 7:15-18, Philippians 2:9-11, Hebrews 12:12-13

Lame (see Feet and Paralytic)

Leprosy (see Skin or Plagues)

Life (includes Live, Lives)

Genesis 6:3, Genesis 15:15, Deuteronomy 11:9, Deuteronomy 30:19-20, Deuteronomy 34:7, Job 5:26, Job 27:3-4, Psalm 16:11, Psalm 23:6, Psalm 24:6, Psalm 25:2, Psalm 27:1-2, Psalm

33:18-19, Psalm 39:4-5, Psalm 90:10, Psalm 91:16, Psalm 92:14, Psalm 116:8-9, Psalm 118:17, Psalm 119:37, Psalm 119:93, Psalm 139:13, Psalm 139:16, Proverbs 3:21-23, Proverbs 4:10, Proverbs 4:20-22, Proverbs 10:12, Proverbs 12:18, Proverbs 15:31, Proverbs 18:21, Proverbs 21:21, Ecclesiastes 3:1-2, Isaiah 38:5-6, Isaiah 38:16-17, Isaiah 43:1-3, Isaiah 46:4, Ezekiel 37:6, Ezekiel 37:9, Ezekiel 37:14, Amos 5:4, Matthew 7:7-9, John 1:4, John 3:16, John 5:24, John 6:57-58, John 10:10, John 11:25, John 11:42-44, John 6:63, Acts 9:40, Acts 17:25, Romans 5:10, Romans 5:21, Romans 6:4, Romans 6:23, Romans 8:2, Romans 14:8-9, 1 Corinthians 15:20-22, Ephesians 6:2-3, 1 Timothy 4:8, 1 Peter 3:10-11, 2 Peter 1:3-4, Revelation 2:7

Love (Includes Loves, Loved)

Psalm 5:11, Psalm 18:1-3, Psalm 45:7, Psalm 119:13, Proverbs 12:1, Proverbs 18:21, Proverbs 22:11, Hosea 14:4, Matthew 22:37-40, Mark 12:29-31, John 3:16, John 14:15, John 14:21, 1 Corinthians 13:4-7, Galatians 2:20, Galatians 5:22-23, Ephesians 4:16, Philippians 2:1-2, Philippians 4:6-8, Colossians 1:13, Colossians 2:2, Colossians 3:14-15, 1 Timothy 6:10, 1 Timothy 6:11-12, 2 Timothy 1:7, 2 Timothy 2:22, 1 John 2:15-16, 1 John 3:17, 1 John 3:21-22, 1 John 4:18, 1 John 4:20-21, 1 John 5:3, Revelation 21:11, Revelation 22:14-16

Mind (see also Thoughts)

Job 38:36, Psalm 1:1-2, Proverbs 3:22-23, Proverbs 9:6, Proverbs 12:1, Proverbs 12:8, Proverbs 12:15-16, Proverbs 13:3, Ecclesiastes 9:17-18, Isaiah 54:13, Jeremiah 17:9-10, Daniel 9:8, Matthew 7:7-9, Matthew 16:23, Matthew 22:37-40, Acts 3:16, Romans 7:22-23, Romans 7:24-25, Romans 12:2, 2 Corinthians 4:3-4, 2 Corinthians 10:3-5, Ephesians 4:17-18, Ephesians 4:22-24, Ephesians 5:26, Philippians 2:1-2, Colossians 2:18-19, 1 Thessalonians 5:5-7, Titus 2:6-8, Titus 2:11-14, James 1:5, James 3:17, James 4:7-8, 1 Peter 3:8-9, 1 Peter 5:7-9

Miscarriage (see Barrenness)

Mourning (see also Grief)

Nehemiah 8:10, Psalm 30:11, Psalm 73:21, Isaiah 57:18, Isaiah 61:1-3, Jeremiah 31:13, Hosea 4:2-3, Revelation 21:4

Mouth (see Voice)

Muscles (includes Sinews)

Ezekiel 37:6, Colossians 2:18-19

Mute (see Voice)

Neck

Deuteronomy 28:47-48, Psalm 73:6, Proverbs 3:21-23, Proverbs 6:20-22, Isaiah 10:27, Matthew 18:6

Oil

Psalm 104:14-15, Psalm 109:17-18, Isaiah 10:27, Isaiah 61:1-3, Mark 6:13, Luke 10:33, James 5:14

Old Age (see Life)

Pain

1 Chronicles 4:10, Psalm 37:17-18, Psalm 55:4-5, Psalm 69:29, Psalm 116:3-4, Isaiah 13:7-8, Isaiah 38:13-14, Jeremiah 15:18-19, Jeremiah 30:15, Revelation 21:4

Paralytic (see also Feet or Lame)

Matthew 4:24, Matthew 9:2, Matthew 9:6-7, Mark 2:3-5, Luke 17:19, John 5:6, John 5:8-9

Peace

Genesis 15:15, Psalm 4:8, Psalm 29:11, Psalm 72:7, Proverbs 14:30, Isaiah 32:18, Isaiah 53:5, Isaiah 54:13, Isaiah 57:19, Jeremiah 29:11, Jeremiah 33:6, John 14:27, John 16:33, Romans 8:6, 1 Corinthians 14:33, Galatians 5:22-23, Philippians 4:6-8, 1 Timothy 6:6, 2 Timothy 2:22, Hebrews 12:12-13, 1 Peter 3:10-11, James 3:17

Plagues (see also Disease)

Exodus 12:13, Leviticus 14:53-55, Deuteronomy 28:58-60, 1 Kings 8:37-39, Psalm 91:10, Isaiah 53:4, Hosea 13:14, Luke 7:21, Revelation 18:4-5

Promise

Deuteronomy 28:1, Deuteronomy 28:15, 1 Kings 8:56, Psalm 1:1-2, Matthew 7:7-9, Matthew 7:10-12, John 14:12-14, John 14:21, Romans 3:4, Romans 4:19-21, 2 Corinthians 1:20, Galatians 3:13-14, Galatians 3:29, Ephesians 6:2-3, 1 Timothy 4:8,

Hebrews 6:11-14, Hebrews 6:17-18, Hebrews 8:6, Hebrews 10:22-23, Hebrews 11:11, James 2:5

Rest (see Sleep)

Restore

Psalm 41:3-4, Isaiah 57:18, Jeremiah 30:17, Matthew 12:10-13, Mark 8:25, Luke 6:10

Resurrection Life (see Death)

Salvation (includes Save)

Exodus 14:13-14, Exodus 15:2, Psalm 18:1-3, Psalm 27:1-2, Psalm 35:9-10, Psalm 69:29, Psalm 91:16, Psalm 106:4-5, Isaiah 12:2-3, Luke 9:56, 2 Corinthians 6:2, 2 Corinthians 7:10, Ephesians 6:16-17, Philippians 1:19, 1 Thessalonians 5:9-10, Titus 2:11-14, Hebrews 9:27-28

Senses (see also Touch)

Hebrews 5:14

Shoulders

Deuteronomy 33:12, Psalm 38:4-5, Isaiah 10:27, Isaiah 14:24-25

Sickness (see also Disease, Plagues, Infirmity)

Exodus 23:25, Deuteronomy 7:15, 1 Kings 8:37-39, 2 Chronicles 21:15, Job 19:20, Psalm 41:3-4, Proverbs 18:14, Isaiah 53:4, Ezekiel 34:16, Matthew 4:23, Matthew 9:35, Mark 2:17, Luke 5:31-32, John 11:4, Acts 5:16, 1 Corinthians 11:29-31, Philippians 2:27

Sin (see Iniquity)

Skin

Leviticus 19:28-29, Job 10:11-12, Job 19:20, Job 30:30, Job 33:24-25, Psalm 38:3, Psalm 38:7, Psalm 73:26, Matthew 8:2-3, Mark 1:40-42, Luke 5:12-13, Luke 7:22

Sleep (includes Rest)

Esther 6:1, Job 33:14-16, Psalm 4:4, Psalm 4:8, Psalm 17:15, Psalm 23:2-3, Psalm 37:7-9, Psalm 91:5-6, Psalm 127:2, Proverbs 3:24, Proverbs

6:20-22, Proverbs 19:15, Isaiah 32:18, Ecclesiastes 5:12, Daniel 2:1, Zechariah 4:1, Matthew 11:28-30, Luke 9:32, Ephesians 5:14, 1 Thessalonians 5:5-7, 1 Thessalonians 5:9-10, Hebrews 4:9-11

Sorrow (see also Mourning)

Job 17:7, Psalm 31:10, Palm 32:10-11, Psalm 34:18, Psalm 39:2-3, Psalm 116:3-4, Psalm 119:28, Proverbs 10:10, Proverbs 23:29-30, Isaiah 13:7-8, Isaiah 35:10, Isaiah 54:4, Jeremiah 3:13, Jeremiah 31:24-26, Hosea 13:12-13, Luke 6:21, 2 Corinthians 7:10, Philippians 2:27, 1 Timothy 6:10

Speak (see Voice)

Spirit

Genesis 6:3, Job 10:11-12, Job 27:3-4, Job 33:4, Psalm 32:1-2, Psalm 51:10, Psalm 77:3, Psalm 143:3, Psalm 143:7-8, Proverbs 15:4, Proverbs 15:13, Proverbs 17:22, Proverbs 18:14, Proverbs 19:15, Proverbs 29:22-25, Isaiah 38:16-17, Isaiah 59:21, Isaiah 61:1-3, Jeremiah 1:5, Ezekiel 36:26, Ezekiel 37:14, Daniel 2:1, Joel 2:28, Matthew 8:15-16, Matthew 26:41, Luke 4:18-19, John 6:63, Acts 2:38, Acts 10:38, Romans 8:1, Romans 8:2, Romans 8:6, Romans 8:9, Romans

8:11, Romans 8:13, Romans 8:26-27, Romans 12:10-13, Romans 15:30, 1 Corinthians 2:3-5, 1 Corinthians 4:13, 1 Corinthians 6:19-20, 1 Corinthians 12:9, 1 Corinthians 15:42-44, Galatians 3:1-3, Galatians 3:13-14, Galatians 5:16, Galatians 5:22-23, Galatians 6:7-9, Ephesians 3:20-21, Ephesians 4:22-24, Ephesians 5:18, Ephesians 6:16-17, Philippians 1:19, Philippians 2:1-2, 2 Thessalonians 2:8, Hebrews 4:12-13, 1 Peter 3:3-4, 1 Peter 4:13-14, 1 John 4:1, Revelation 2:7, Revelation 22:17

Spiritual Warfare (see also Demons)

Matthew 6:10-13, Matthew 10:1, Matthew 10:8, Matthew 13:49-50, Matthew 16:23, Matthew 17:15-18, Matthew 18:18

Stomach (see Bowels)

Strength

Deuteronomy 33:25, Job 6:14, Psalm 12:5, Psalm 18:1-3, Psalm 18:32-34, Psalm 27:1-2, Psalm 29:11, Psalm 31:10, Psalm 89:20, Psalm 103:4-5, Psalm 118:6-7, Psalm 105:37, Psalm 119:28, Proverbs 24:10-12, Isaiah 12:2-3, Isaiah 40:29, Isaiah 40:31, Isaiah 41:10, Isaiah 41:13, Jeremiah 16:19,

Ezekiel 34:16, Joel 3:10, Matthew 22:37-40, Acts 3:16, Romans 8:26-27, 1 Corinthians 11:29-31, 2 Corinthians 12:9-10, Ephesians 3:20-21, Philippians 4:13, Colossians 1:10-11, Colossians 3:20-21, Hebrews 11:32-34, Revelation 3:10

Stress (see Anxiety)

Stumble (see Feet)

Thoughts (includes Thinking, Wisdom)

Job 38:36, Psalm 39:2-3, Psalm 94:19, Psalm 119:25, Psalm 119:65-67, Psalm 119:113, Psalm 139:23, Proverbs 6:20-22, Proverbs 12:8, Proverbs 12:15-16, Proverbs 14:12, Proverbs 16:2, Proverbs 24:13-14, Proverbs 26:8-9, Jeremiah 29:11, Luke 7:7, 2 Corinthians 10:3-5, Philippians 3:13, Philippians 4:6-8, Colossians 1:10-11, Colossians 2:2, 1 Timothy 1:18-20, 2 Timothy 2:24-26, 2 Timothy 3:7

Tongue (see Voice)

Torment

Matthew 4:24, Matthew 18:34, Acts 5:16, Revelation 14:11

Touch

Matthew 8:2-3, Matthew 8:15-16, Matthew 9:21, Matthew 9:28-30, Matthew 14:35-36, Mark 1:40-42, Mark 3:10, Mark 6:56, Luke 5:12-13, Luke 6:19, Luke 8:47

Victory

1 Chronicles 29:11-12, Proverbs 16:3, Proverbs 21:31, Ecclesiastes 3:6, Isaiah 43:1-3, Jeremiah 17:7, Malachi 3:11, Matthew 7:7-9, John 16:33, Romans 8:31, 1 Corinthians 15:57, 1 John 5:4

Voice

Job 27:3-4, Psalm 5:9, Psalm 12:2-4, Psalm 16:9, Psalm 17:9-10, Psalm 19:14, Psalm 26:6-7, Psalm 32:10-11, Psalm 39:2-3, Psalm 40:2-3, Psalm 63:3-4, Psalm 63:5, Psalm 66:16-19, Psalm 77:3, Psalm 78:36-42, Psalm 102:3-5, Psalm 106:4-5, Psalm 119:170-173, Psalm 145:21, Psalm 149:6-9, Proverbs 10:12, Proverbs 10:18-20, Proverbs 12:13-14, Proverbs 12:18, Proverbs 13:3, Proverbs 15:4, Proverbs 22:11, Proverbs 25:15, Proverbs 26:2, Proverbs 26:6-7, Proverbs 26:8-9, Proverbs 30:14,

Ecclesiastes 9:17-18, Isaiah 32:4, Isaiah 35:6, Isaiah 59:21, Matthew 8:8, Matthew 9:32-33, Matthew 12:22, Matthew 15:29-31, Mark 7:33-35, Mark 9:17, Mark 9:25, Luke 7:7, Luke 11:14, Acts 2:26, 2 Corinthians 4:13, 2 Corinthians 7:4, Ephesians 3:20-21, Colossians 3:5-8, Colossians 3:20-21, 2 Thessalonians 2:8, 1 Timothy 1:18-20, 1 Timothy 6:11-12, 2 Timothy 2:24-26, Titus 2:6-8, Titus 3:10-11, Hebrews 10:22-23, Hebrews 10:35, James 1:26-27, James 3:6, James 3:8, James 5:9, 1 Peter 3:8-9, 1 Peter 3:10-11

Weakness (see Strength)

Weariness (see Strength)

Whole

Job 5:18, Proverbs 4:20-22, Malachi 3:10, Matthew 12:10-13, Matthew 14:35-36, James 3:6

Wisdom (see Thoughts)

Words (see Voice)

Worry (see Anxiety)

Wound/Wounds

Deuteronomy 33:12, Job 5:18, Psalm 38:4-5, Psalm 89:31-32, Psalm 109:22-24, Psalm 147:3, Proverbs 7:23, Proverbs 12:18, Proverbs 30:14, Isaiah 1:4-6, Isaiah 30:26, Isaiah 53:5, Jeremiah 15:18-19, Jeremiah 30:17, Hosea 6:1, Luke 10:33-34, Colossians 3:20-21, 1 Peter 2:24

Can You Help?

I appreciate feedback, and I love hearing what readers have to say. Your input helps to make subsequent versions of this book and future books better. Please leave an honest book review letting me know what you thought of the book. Share your favorite quote or share a photo or video.

There's a whole community praying for God's healing hand to touch every reader, and we'd love to praise the Lord with you to celebrate your victory! If you have a testimony of healing to share, please email FirebrandUnited@gmail.com.

Thanks so much!

Sallie Dawkins

Also by This Author

The three-part, best-selling **Awakening Christian Series** shares Sallie Dawkins' testimony of discovering identity, potential, and purpose in Christ. A heart encounter with God in 2015 challenged Sallie's entire belief system. It was the beginning of the end of two-and-a-half decades of wavering faith and started her on a supernatural journey of discovery that rapidly transformed her life. Now an ordained Christian healing evangelist, Sallie teaches through testimony, inviting born-again Christians to confront assumptions, doubts, and lies.

The Awakening Christian Series is a valuable tool for guiding believers into a more meaningful relationship with God and answers questions Christians can't, don't, or won't ask in church. If we don't know or believe that God is who He says He is, how will we ever know or receive the fullness of His love for us? And if we cannot love ourselves and who we are in Christ, how will we love others as they deserve to be loved?

The lessons Sallie shares about her journey of spiritual growth can benefit every born-again Christian. This series is suitable for individuals and small groups. Readers will find valuable resources and application questions at the end of each chapter. Sallie Dawkins will show you how God brought healing to her own life, and how He can do it for you, too!

Printed in Great Britain
by Amazon

83118612R00122